HOW TO PROSPER IN THE UNDERGROUND ECONOMY

HOW TO PROSPER IN THE UNDERGROUND ECONOMY

A Completely Legal Guide to the hidden, multibillion-dollar cash economy . . . the barter exchange network . . . independence and security during the coming currency collapse . . . winning with investments in the uncertain 80's . . . capitalizing on economic self-help groups . . . exploiting individual entrepreneurial opportunities

Larry Burkett
with William Proctor

WILLIAM MORROW AND COMPANY, INC.
New York   *1982*

Library of Congress Cataloging in Publication Data

Burkett, Larry.
   How to prosper in the underground economy.

   1. Informal sector (Economics)—Handbooks,
manuals, etc.   2. Finance (Personal)—Handbooks,
manuals, etc.   I. Proctor, William.   II. Title.
HD2341.B87   332.024   81-14172
ISBN 0-688-00778-3   AACR2

Printed in the United States of America

First Edition

1 2 3 4 5 6 7 8 9 10

BOOK DESIGN BY MICHAEL MAUCERI

To my wife, Judy,
and my children, Larry, Dan, Todd and Kim

CONTENTS

HOW TO PROSPER

HOW TO PROSPER IN THE UNDERGROUND ECONOMY

CHAPTER ONE

Do You Really Need a Cabin in the Woods and Dehydrated Food?

Many individual Americans are now on the verge of serious financial troubles. And as the months and years roll on, the troubles are going to get worse and more widespread—primarily because of inescapable economic forces and conditioned personal habits that are hard, if not impossible, to change.

Like a growing number of other economists and business analysts, I believe that inflation, caused by unchecked government spending and combined with a lack of individual financial discipline, is moving us steadily toward a devastating money crisis. But unlike many "crisis" prognosticators, I *don't* think it's necessary to store guns, gold and food and hide out in the mountains in order to survive. If such radical steps are the only haven from the

13

coming economic storms, then all but the very rich—and eccentric—are in big trouble.

You don't have to take such drastic measures to survive and to prosper. During the past several years, I've devoted much time to studying economic trends and gathering information in practical financial counseling sessions with thousands of individuals and families from a wide variety of geographical, occupational and income backgrounds. Such evidence suggests strongly that if you begin to plan *now*, you can sidestep the seemingly inevitable monetary collapse—and do it in style. But you can't just sit back and hope that the economic problems will go away or that somehow the current "quick fix" advocated by politicians will resolve the problem. You must develop a personal financial plan and begin to act on it *immediately*. My function is to help you develop the plan; yours is to *act* on it.

But there's more to an effective personal money plan these days than just planning for a crisis. First, you must continue to carry on your daily business regardless of any pending crisis; so any meaningful program must take into account day-to-day living (not merely existing in the future somewhere in a survival hideout).

And secondly, since there is always the possibility that there won't be a total collapse, no plan should be completely dependent on a crisis. It may be that all of the catastrophe predictions, including my own, will be negated by rational government economics in the future. If the future economic scenario turns out to be fade-out instead of burn-out, you'd feel pretty silly making payments on a fortified cabin in the woods and munching on dehydrated food.

Please don't misunderstand: I do believe there will be a

monetary collapse. In fact, I think it's *inevitable*, unless an unforeseen war or similar earthshaking event occurs. The structure of our money system and indeed our entire economy will undergo a dramatic change by the mid-1980's. We're riding in a boat headed for the waterfall, and our government is the helmsman. The only thing that can alter our direction is very rapid back-paddling. Otherwise, public fear will require massive government intervention that will remove the last vestige of private enterprise.

If such a collapse does occur, it is vital for you to have made personal financial preparations to provide for yourself and your family. If it doesn't occur, the worst that can happen is that you have a sound financial plan that will accommodate any economy we may have in the future.

By now you may be saying, "This is too much hedging. Nobody can have it both ways—a plan that will work if there is a collapse or if there isn't." But actually, you *can* have it both ways, and in fact, any plan that won't help you prosper in any economy is terribly shortsighted. The investments may change, but the source of wisdom never does. There is a set of universal, timeless economic principles that must serve as the basis for any successful personal financial plan. But unfortunately, in our society those principles have become obscured in recent years.

The ensuing pages will reveal how to arrange your finances so that you and your family are in a stronger position to deal with financial challenges, no matter what the state of the national economy. Along the way you'll learn about a system of personal economic planning advocated as early as the biblical Book of Genesis and actually used by some of the ancient Hebrews to get their own financial affairs in order.

This is called the *underground economy*. And it will

soon become evident that it is a viable way to reduce living costs and expand your assets.

What exactly is the underground economy? You'll have the full picture of what it involves as you get further into this book. But for now, you can think of it as being an economic system that operates *outside* our normal system of economics. It's a kind of "system within a system," a network of exchange and transaction that is largely insulated from the ups and downs that play havoc with our economy. In fact, the worse our regular system gets, the better the underground system gets.

The underground economy is also a noncash network of buying and selling that is *completely legal*. There is an illegal underground economy, and we'll discuss that in some detail later, too. But the illegal system is not what you want—because it ultimately leads to fear and frustration, rather than to peace and prosperity. My counsel is limited to the legal techniques for organizing personal finances.

Contrary to some "take care of yourself and nobody else" notions of setting up a financial and investment plan, the underground economy way is rooted firmly in comprehensive community involvement as well as in creative personal money management programs. Here are a few of the specifics:

• The legal underground economy is based solidly on a *community system of sharing goods and services*. Many of the so-called "doomsday" economic prophets suggest ways of preparing for a collapse that are thoroughly selfish and anticommunity-oriented. Fleeing to the woods with an armload of guns to hold off your neighbors is about as far from a moral plan as one can imagine—not to mention the fact that it won't work for 98 percent of the population.

But you can go a long way toward insulating yourself from economic setbacks if you develop channels of community support in the underground economy, such as barter arrangements, food cooperatives and other sharing strategies. This aspect of the underground economy really is *under* ground in the sense that many Americans aren't aware of it. You can be certain that official government agencies like the Internal Revenue Service would like to know more about it—primarily to be able to regulate or tax it.

But these community sharing networks are so decentralized and difficult to oversee that there's little likelihood the government will be able to gain any control over them. And that's what the underground economy's all about: It's largely protected from government interference —and as a result, also protected from restrictive measures the government may take during a national economic crisis. This book will describe in detail how you can get into a community sharing setup and thereby ensure that your line of financial defense will stand up regardless of what happens in the economy.

• To make the best use of the underground economy, it's absolutely essential that you get your personal finances in order, and that means (1) establishing a special kind of easy-to-maintain *crisis budget* and (2) resolving to take a *radical approach to personal debt*. The purpose of paying such close attention to your personal finances is twofold: to strengthen your family's financial position while the economy is still sound, and also to enable you to generate

17

a surplus—which you can put into "crisis-proof" investments that will bolster your finances even more firmly.

• Also, as part of your involvement in the underground economy, you should investigate the *alternative job market*. This means to choose a hobby or a part-time job that can be transformed into a full-blown self-employment enterprise, if need be. This option will provide you with an excellent hedge against inflation and also a great insurance policy in times of high unemployment. Thousands of people around the country are training themselves in this phase of the underground economy, and in the following pages you'll learn what steps you need to take to do the same.

• Perhaps the most glamorous and potentially most lucrative part of your participation in the underground economy will be the development of a personal portfolio of *crisis-proof investments*. Most of these investment opportunities are "above" ground in the sense that many investors already use them as a regular part of their portfolios. Actually, anyone can purchase them by going to a knowledgeable broker, agent or seller. But what isn't widely known is how to select these collapse-proof investments from the myriad of other investments that would not survive a monetary collapse. You'll discover how people in a variety of different personal economic positions need to invest their money, and learn some specific guidelines to help you come up with your own balanced, collapse-proof portfolio.

Getting into the underground economy, then, doesn't require a commitment to some sort of strange, eccentric life-style, nor does it involve an obsession with gold or dehydrated foods. In order to take full advantage of this largely invisible, low-profile economic system, you must acquire some additional economic knowledge and skills. You'll also have to be willing to do more than just read this book. This is not an academic exercise. It's a practical action plan that will benefit you *only* if you're willing to start changing some of your present financial habits and views and take the risk of trying something entirely new.

If you do decide to plunge into the underground economy, I can assure you of this: *You can't lose.* If there is no monetary collapse, the worst thing that will happen is that you'll be debt free, have a workable budget and have a viable investment plan that will top anything others are doing. Additionally, you will be actively involved in a community sharing plan with other families of similar values. You'll learn some new practical skills that will save you money and give you a sense of personal accomplishment.

But if there *is* a collapse, the underground system will provide basic family needs, security and even prosperity.

As yet we've only scratched the surface. Now, let's get down to the specifics of where the underground economy comes from, where it's going and what you can do to participate in it.

CHAPTER TWO

What Is the Underground Economy?

Americans are far too optimistic. Most were either born into affluence or have enjoyed it for so long that they can't imagine really hard times.

These assumptions about the certainty of American affluence have created a dangerous illusion of economic security where there really is no security. In fact, we're moving swiftly toward a financial waterfall, and there is no way we can avoid tumbling over the edge. Many Americans will wake up one day to find that their retirement plans, their investments and their other assets have been effectively destroyed, first by inflation, then deflation caused by a worthless money system.

But others—those who recognize the coming cataclysms and act now to prepare themselves—will make a soft landing and find they are actually in better shape than they were before the monetary collapse. Those who make it unscathed through the future economic crisis must, for the most part, have a better understanding than average of where our economy has been and where it's going. We must either learn from history or be doomed to repeat it.

So the first thing for us to do is review some information which is vitally important to provide a better understanding of the present and perhaps a glimpse of the future. Once you have this full scenario in mind, you may well come to the same conclusion that I have: Because we are heading toward a monetary collapse in the United States, it's absolutely imperative that each individual take steps right now to recapture and put into practice some of the fundamental economic principles that put our ancestors on the road to personal financial freedom.

First, let's go back to those early days when the American colonies were struggling to survive. One approach that England and Spain tried was to establish trade companies designed to ship criminals and debtors over to the colonies to work the land, glean its resources and then send the goods back to the mother countries. These ventures turned out to be abysmal failures because the conscripted labor, with no share in the profits and little prospect for advancement, lacked economic motivation.

But then Governor William Bradford of the Plymouth colony, who had been facing the same problems that plagued others in the New World, got an idea: He formed a *free enterprise economy*. Specifically, he took every individual under him who wanted to work and gave that person several acres of land to farm. He said, in effect, "You grow everything you can on that land, give the company its portion and keep the rest."

Bradford quickly found that those with only a few acres

of privately owned land could out-produce those with many more acres who were working only for the trade company. Here's the way he put it in his *Of Plymouth Plantation 1620–1647*:

". . . no supply was heard of [by the Plymouth colonists in 1623], neither knew they when they might expect any. So they began to think how they might raise as much corn as they could, and obtain a better crop than they had done, that they might not still thus languish in misery. At length, after much debate of things, the Governor . . . assigned to every family a parcel of land, according to the proportion of their number. . . . This had very good success, for it made all hands industrious. . . ."

A similar kind of work ethic was eventually tried in other American colonies, and the concept spread and became the foundation for our system of private land ownership and free enterprise. Of course, not every attempt at this new economic approach worked perfectly —but those that failed usually fell short because they didn't go far enough.

In the Jamestown colony of Virginia, for example, Captain John Smith became exasperated upon seeing his colony failing because of lazy noblemen and other goldbrickers. So he laid down a law, based on the Apostle Paul's command in Second Thessalonians 3:10: ". . . he that will not work shall not eat (except by sickness he be disabled) for the labors of thirty or forty honest and industrious men shall not be consumed to an hundred and fifty idle loiterers. . . . Therefore he that offendeth, let him assuredly expect his due punishment."

But there were serious limits on what Smith could do to instill a work ethic and entrepreneurial drive in the colonists because, among other things, the society lacked a system of free land ownership. So Jamestown was eventually abandoned. But many other colonies began to succeed, and the basic foundation was laid for our nation to later become the greatest industrial power on earth.

In addition to this developing free enterprise orientation, there were other important factors that made our young nation economically strong.

One key feature of our society in those days was a *firm family foundation* that encouraged each family member to participate vigorously and knowledgeably in meaningful work. Children were trained from an early age in their responsibilities to the family economy, whether it was operating a plow, keeping the accounting books or babysitting. Elderly family members also remained productive well into their later years.

Another thing that helped those early entrepreneurs was the existence of *community cooperative plans*. Each family knew that if it ran into trouble due to crop failure or illness, it could turn to other families in the area for help.

Also, our nation was founded on a network of *local governments*, with national influences remaining largely in the background. There was a major advantage to this decentralized kind of political organization because as different industries sprang up around the country, each community formulated the laws that were best suited to nurturing local business.

But ironically, these strong beginnings had in them the seeds of their own downfall, for they led us directly into prosperity. Prosperity, in turn, produced economic and political power centers. And these power centers eventually overshadowed or destroyed the very foundations that had made it possible for us to become the greatest industrial power the world had ever seen. The problem we now face is the very real danger of forfeiting the prosperity we have worked so hard to achieve—all because we've turned our backs on those values and practices that originally made us so successful.

What we now call the underground economy is actually nothing more than a contemporary version of the traditional economy of our forefathers. Getting into the underground economy involves returning to our roots—roots which have been damaged and devastated mercilessly throughout this century.

What specifically are those values we have lost but hope to recapture by entering the underground economy? Here are a few of the major ones:

We've lost the support and power of the small community. Our telephones, televisions and jet airplanes may have brought us closer together in terms of communication and travel. But they haven't brought us any closer in spirit.

Also, the increased power of the federal government has played a major role in undercutting the power of the local community. No longer are our neighbors' needs accepted as our responsibility. Instead, we look to the government as the primary source of assistance.

This fact struck home with me when I read the results of a nationwide survey for which I was asked to submit several questions. One of the questions was whether people felt they could rely on the federal government if they had an accident that disabled them. An overwhelming 97 percent said yes. But when asked if they could

25

rely on their own church in the event of such a disablement, only .5 percent replied in the affirmative.

We've lost the ability to trade with one another in an environment free of excessive governmental regulation. People today are literally being driven out of business because of the onerous burden of government forms they have to fill out. It's very hard for small entrepreneurs to break into the economy at all today—as they are overwhelmed with requirements like complex income tax forms, safety requirements and a multitude of specific standards that apply to each industry. One of the goals of the underground economy is to provide you with channels of economic exchange that sidestep, as much as is legally possible, these heavy governmental regulations.

We've lost the desire to work hard. Many people aren't interested in working hard because they no longer feel in control of their jobs, and they sense an impersonal atmosphere about their responsibilities. Involvement in big corporations and big labor movements has brought us high wages and attractive fringe benefits—but also an empty feeling that the contributions of one individual don't amount to much. As you learn how to "work underground" on a smaller scale, however, as part of the self-employed alternative job market, you'll see that it's possible to recapture the joy of achievement that motivated many of our forebears.

We've lost a sound monetary system. Perhaps most devastating of all, we've drifted away from the sound personal, business and governmental financial practices that made us great. Through excessive use of credit and unwise budgeting practices, both on a personal and a national level, we've put ourselves on the brink of a monetary disaster.

To understand the full import of this problem, let's pick up the story of our economy in the early part of this century and see where the historical forces that were building then are now leading us.

CHAPTER THREE

Surviving the Great Currency Collapse

We've seen how certain forces have been at work to undercut the foundations of our free enterprise economy. The erosion of the economy in recent years through inflation and taxation has motivated many individuals to try to recapture those original, foundational principles in what we'll be describing throughout this book as the underground economy.

But there is another, even more ominous set of factors at work in our society that makes it absolutely imperative that you get out of the paper money economy and into the underground economy before time runs out. I'm referring to the strong possibility—indeed, in my opinion, the *inevitability*—of a monetary collapse in the United States.

But let me clarify a couple of things before I pursue this line of argument any further. First of all, I'm talking about a *monetary* collapse—a crisis that destroys the viability of our currency—and *not* a general economic collapse.

There's a big difference between the two because in an economic collapse the very foundations of production and employment grind to a halt, while in a monetary collapse it is the financial base of the economic system that falls apart.

To get the full picture, it's necessary to go back a number of years, to the first part of this century. We actually began to create our present predicament as early as the end of World War I. Before 1917, we were in many respects an isolated nation, not involved in world politics or the protection of other nations to any significant degree. We didn't feel it was our responsibility to protect the rest of the world and in fact, we concentrated on the development of our own resources.

One thing that quickly set us apart from all other nations was our industrial productivity. We outstripped everybody else in the output of war materials, and because we didn't have to do any fighting on our own soil, we came out of the conflict stronger than any other nation.

The Europeans, looking at how successful we had been, leaned heavily on our resources to revitalize their war-torn economies, and we responded to their call for help. But unfortunately, we didn't take the system that had worked so well for us and implant it in their lives. Instead, we took a brand-new, untested theory that has been associated with the economist John Maynard Keynes and sent some academicians over to Europe to field-test the concept.

For purposes of this discussion, you can assume that the academic world of economics is divided into two camps —the free-market monetarists and the Keynesians. The monetarists, who basically affirm those economic principles that were with us from the early days of the American Republic, believe that the government shouldn't meddle with the natural course of the economy. If the economy is on a downswing, you let it stay down because it will recover by itself and be stronger in the long run as weak businesses are weeded out and unproductive workers are shifted to other jobs. The monetarists also believe in keeping the money supply stable by affixing its value to a standard such as gold, so that paper money doesn't proliferate and thereby cause increased inflation—hence, their name, monetarist.

The Keynesians, on the other hand, believe that it's the government's prime responsibility to manipulate the money supply during economic downturns and thus to stabilize the situation to keep unemployment as low as possible. In other words, it's as much the government's obligation as the individual's to see that the individual stays employed.

So, Keynes said, the government should borrow to inject money into the economy to stimulate it during bad times and then repay the loans out of surpluses during good times. That's fine, in theory. But in practice, governments that have tried to implement Keynes's ideas have been quick to borrow and slow to pay back. They have also been too ready to print or create new money when the economy becomes sluggish.

Such was the case with the Weimar Republic in Germany, the first regime to be established there after World War I. American economists, with their untried and unproven Keynesian theories, were turned loose to assist in the economic recovery plan. The problem in Europe was that the need for money was unlimited, but the supply of hard currency woefully limited. Rather than using gold as the fixed standard of value, our professors

31

decided to print paper money, deutsche marks, on a "float-ing" exchange basis. Unfortunately, the marks didn't float —they sank.

In 1918, the mark traded on the German exchange for about nine marks per dollar. But because the economists and politicians failed to control the supply of paper money diligently, the value of the marks soon began to erode at an alarming rate. By early 1921, as the presses continued to turn out more money, the German mark had been so devalued that a dollar was now worth a million marks. A few months later the dollar was worth billions of marks.

The Weimar Republic soon collapsed, and for about five years Germany lapsed into what we would now call a depression. The promise of recovery appeared in the form of a government known as the Third Reich—the basic premise of which was, "We'll stabilize the economy for you." And they did stabilize it, under the leadership of Adolf Hitler.

So the Keynesian economic philosophy failed totally in post-World War I Germany, but the economists who had been trying vainly to establish their theories there came home eager to try again. Surprisingly, American politi-cians quickly forgot how these academicians had failed so miserably. Why? For one thing, the Keynesian theory is quite seductive in that it holds out a tantalizing promise of the good life, general affluence, happiness and reelection.

The quickest way to national wealth and well-being, the Keynesian argument goes, is to give the federal govern-ment free rein in providing for your needs. The problem is that in order to provide goods and services, the govern-ment needs money, and that means taking it from ordi-nary citizens by printing more of it or by raising taxes. Because a national income tax had been authorized by the

Sixteenth Amendment to the U.S. Constitution in 1913, the federal government now had all the tools it needed to enter our individual lives in a revolutionary way. So with the Great Depression of the 1930's providing the impetus, our national leaders started us down a road of excessive government spending and poor money management that has finally put us on the verge of a monetary collapse.

From a national debt that was practically nonexistent at the beginning of the twentieth century, we moved up to $16 billion in the 1920's, to $270 billion by the end of World War II, to $300 billion by 1960, to $400 billion by 1970 and finally to a trillion dollars by the early 1980's. The interest on the debt has escalated to the point where now we must borrow more money each year just to pay the interest.

I often think of our present-day economy in terms of a ship with a gaping eight-foot hole in the bottom, and for the longest time there was nobody on top even trying to pump out the water that was pouring in. The hole is the trillion-dollar national debt we have hanging over us, and the water rushing through that hole, making it bigger each year, is the budget deficit we run annually—a deficit that may run $50 billion a year or more.

In 1980 we elected a president who started the pump going and slowed the sinking. Through huge cuts in federal spending programs we reduced the amount of water coming into the ship. But unfortunately, we have a six-inch pump trying to keep up with an eight-foot hole. Each year, that hole—the national debt—gets larger as the existing debt comes due at a higher interest rate. And in just a few years, according to my calculations, the hole is going to get so large that the ship will sink.

In other words, our money will most likely be worthless,

and we'll have to start all over again with an entirely new ship—a new economic order based on a completely different approach to money and individual business transactions.

The disturbing thing about all this is that there doesn't seem to be any way an American President with even the best of intentions can save our economic ship. A chief executive who works consistently over several years to cut federal spending and then to cut taxes to encourage more investing can delay the final currency collapse. And an intervening event, like a major war, might put off the inevitable even longer. But there seems to be little hope of avoiding a collapse in the long run.

Unfortunately, individual citizens and businesses these days have started following the lead of the government in the use of credit. But as Dr. Ludwig von Mises, a leading monetarist at the first part of this century, once said, "Credit is like a tiger, and the man who rides on the back of a tiger can never get off." That's exactly what's happened both to the federal government and also to many American families.

In 1928, for example, only 2 percent of the homes constructed in the United States had any debt attached to them; 98 percent were completely debt free. But by 1968, that situation had precisely flipflopped, with 98 percent of our homes being encumbered by mortgages and only 2 percent free of debt. This same trend is evident in other areas of our economy as well. In 1928, if you wanted to buy a car, you had to pay the total amount in cash to the seller. But by 1968, once again about 90 percent of all cars were being purchased on an installment buying plan.

Recent studies also show that about 60 percent of American families have borrowed more money than they *can or will* repay during their lifetimes. About 30 percent have borrowed more than they can *conveniently* repay as each monthly installment comes due. And about 20 percent have borrowed more than they can *possibly* repay out of their current incomes. In other words, these last families must actually borrow more money to make payments on money they have previously borrowed.

The nation's businesses have joined right in with government and private individuals in this credit movement so that now our entire money system is in a precarious state. Our government is more than a trillion dollars in debt. The nation's businesses are leveraged and mortgaged to the hilt. And individual families are way out on a limb on credit.

But why, you might ask, can't we just learn to live with heavy debt and an accompanying high inflation rate?

A major problem with high inflation in any country, and the United States is no exception, is that it gets harder and harder for the government to control the cost of money. The result is a decline in general economic stability because the average citizen and business doesn't know what the next loan or even the next loaf of bread will cost. You can't carry on reasonable business or personal planning if you don't have any idea what goods and services will cost in the future.

So people and businesses begin to live only in the present, borrowing as much as they can with the idea that they will repay what they owe in "cheaper dollars." We are reaching this point right now, and I believe we're on the verge of the following frightening scenario, which will likely unfold as we move further into the 1980's:

The inflation rate will continue to fluctuate somewhat. But even though it will periodically dip into the single-figure range, the long-run trend will be steadily upward—to at least a 15 percent base rate for the early 1980's and 20 percent or even higher later.

When it seems that the economy is out of control, the government will step in to dry up the money supply temporarily through excessively high interest rates. As credit dries up, the weakest companies fail because they can't borrow money to produce their goods or meet their payrolls. When this cycle repeats often enough, recessions start occurring every year and then every few months, with more wage earners joining the hard-core unemployed.

As the unemployment rate goes up, perhaps to 10 percent or 12 percent, many of those who are out of work will find they can't repay their debts—because, remember, even when employed they relied on credit just to meet their monthly living expenses. In addition, creditors who don't get paid also face unemployment.

So a chain reaction begins to build, with increasing personal and business bankruptcies. Banks will also start to go out of business as they can't collect their outstanding loans. The Federal Deposit Insurance Corporation and the Federal Savings and Loan Insurance Corporation will abandon weaker banks in order to save the stronger because there will be only enough money in reserve to cover about 1 percent of the total bank deposits. A hard-pressed federal government is not about to step in during a crisis to make up the difference—no matter how certain some wishful thinkers are that this will occur.

Then, when the epidemic of financial disasters reaches national proportions, the federal government will realize that the American monetary system is no longer viable. The government must intervene and establish a new economic order or be faced with total economic collapse and full-fledged revolution in the cities. At this point, those who have merged into the underground economy will find that they are able both to meet their own needs and to help many others as well.

Now, let's take a closer look at this new economic order and begin to consider some of the practical implications for your personal finances.

First of all, any currency collapse, which is accompanied by high unemployment, is likely to result in some degree of *civil disorder*. Violence is just beneath the surface in many of our major cities, and it's frightening to imagine what might happen if our unemployment rate doubled and the middle class joined poorer people in being unable to buy food for their families. If the choice is between a person's raiding a local grocery store and seeing his children go hungry, I'm afraid the grocer will lose out every time.

It seems highly unlikely that violence and looting could last more than a couple of weeks—or a month at the most. The federal government would certainly step in to restore order, to provide food, medical care and other necessities and also to revamp the nation's monetary system. The final result would be a new economic order that would be quite unlike anything we know today.

One of the most striking features of this new order will be the appearance of a *cashless society*. After a currency collapse, our money would be virtually worthless, so the government would have to create new money. As the trend in recent years has been a shift to some form of "electronic" currency, this would seem to be a characteristic of the economy of the future. Thus, instead of having $10,000 in the bank, you might have 10,000 "digits."

The Federal Reserve System shifts money from member

bank to member bank in somewhat this manner now. Also, those of you who rely on credit cards for many of your purchases know it's not necessary to carry cash around to buy goods and services. You just walk in with your plastic "money," the salesperson puts your card in a machine connected to a central terminal to see if your credit is good, and then if you pass the test, you buy whatever you like up to the limit of your credit. An identification card issued for your "electronic money" account would perform a similar kind of function. But unlike our present credit system, purchases could easily be limited to "cash" available. Not only would this system reduce bank robberies (no cash), but it would make all income and expenditures completely visible to the federal government.

All existing savings accounts, other bank deposits, treasury bills and most other fixed assets—except those necessary to carry on the most basic day-to-day transactions—would likely be frozen indefinitely under the new economic regime. Depositors would still own these accounts in theory, but withdrawal would be limited to the conditions established by the government. Under the guise of "stabilization," personal assets held in financial institutions might well be frozen indefinitely.

Another feature of the new economic order will, in my opinion, be the *decline of gold* as a safe haven from the economic storms. It seems unlikely that gold will ever again be used as a standard of exchange, and in fact, I think the federal government is likely to confiscate it. It's quite possible that we could return to the situation that existed earlier this century, when the possession of gold, except in limited amounts as jewelry, was illegal.

An even more radical departure from past economic practice would be a *prohibition on buying land, automo-*

38

*biles or any other substantial property without govern-
mental approval.* One of the reasons for this strict control
would be to "stabilize" the economy through controlled
spending. In the past such purchases, motivated by easy
credit, contributed to the inflationary spiral and eventually
to the weakening of the monetary system. Any government in power after a currency collapse is not likely to
allow such a practice to continue and will probably go
overboard to ensure a stable currency.

Far-fetched, you think? Not if you will take a good hard
look at our current situation and the terrifying effects a
collapse could have. Then look at the "solutions" from a
political perspective and outline the choices that the politicians are most likely to make. With these considerations
in mind, the shape of the future looks grim indeed.

Now the American people are neither able nor willing
to suffer a complete *economic* collapse or a "stagflation
depression," with high inflation *and* high unemployment.
We're not the same kind of nation we were back in the
1930's. We've come to expect more of the material things
of life, and many people would prefer to overthrow the
government before doing without adequate food and shelter for any period. The alternative scenario of a cashless
society, with close controls over business transactions and
the accumulation of personal wealth, will seem far prefer-
able to voters and politicians alike.

So what does all this have to do with you and your personal finances right now?

First of all, I think it's important to understand the
likely direction of our economy so that you can choose a
personal financial plan that will get you successfully
through any currency crisis. But secondly, a good plan
should also help you in the present, before any possible

crisis occurs. A complete approach to personal money management must take into account crisis-proof investments, the security of your work, your family budget, your access to adequate food supplies, and perhaps most important of all, the strength of your economic ties to others in community self-help programs.

As we embark on a discussion of these principles—which, if followed, can beyond any doubt make you financially secure in the present and into the foreseeable future—we move into the very heart of this book, which centers on the practical operation of the underground economy in the United States.

Now, let's examine what the underground economy really involves, and how getting into it can dramatically increase your surplus of funds now and in the years to come.

CHAPTER FOUR

Plugging into the Underground Economy

The underground economy that we'll be exploring was not always underground.

On the contrary, as we've seen in the brief historical sketch presented earlier, the economic network that today is under the surface of our regular financial and business transactions was once our regular, above-ground economy. Let's look back again for a moment to the formative years of our nation, before the federal government started intervening in a significant way in our personal affairs and before huge corporations and unions began replacing individual enterprise and initiative. In those days there were several key features that characterized our working lives:

First, people were *more concerned about basic survival* than they are now because, in times of crop failure, natural disaster or other unexpected calamity, they might find themselves without enough food to put on the table. This specter of potential starvation made most people conscious of the need for some kind of reliable emergency supplies to tide them over until they could recover from any economic disaster that might occur.

Other nations, of course, are much more sensitive to this survival question because they haven't enjoyed the affluence we have had in the United States. But even in our own country, seemingly well-protected middle-class families often face crises that bring to focus the realities of just how fragile our affluence really is. Even a temporary hardship such as a layoff or illness often catches families unprepared and places unbearable strains on many individuals to the point of suicide or divorce. In our generation, no less than in those of an earlier time, it is imperative for those who make up the heart of our country, middle-income Americans, to seriously consider how they would make it through even a few weeks if the "system" stopped supplying even the very basics of life.

Our ancestors in the American colonies—at least those who survived—learned to make do on a *minimum of income.* They watched their income and expenses very closely and made the best use of every cent or shilling they had because they often didn't know where the next one was coming from.

In other words, they knew how to budget their personal finances, and their children learned at an early age the meaning of money too, primarily because there just wasn't very much of it. As a result, they treated the first dollar as wisely as they did the last. They earned a reputation for being a thrifty people, and a nation that was made up of practical, hard-headed business experts.

In the early days of our country, most people were involved in *small, independently owned businesses*—often they were sole proprietorships that had few, if any, employees. In fact, many of the first business ventures were family undertakings, with most of the workers related by blood.

Today, of course, the situation is completely different. Most people work for companies with remote corporate ownership. These are large by early American standards, and there is little independence or personal initiative, either in terms of setting work hours or defining duties.

Up to the time of the American Revolution, *strong local community ties* were the order of the day. Neighbors helped neighbors in economic trouble, each knowing the other would help in return. This concept was a direct application of a principle taught in every rural American church of those days: ". . . at this present time your abundance being a supply for their want, that their abundance also may become a supply for your want, that there may be equality; as it is written, 'He who gathered much did not have too much, and he who gathered little had no lack.'" (2 Cor. 8:14–15, New American Standard Bible)

In colonial times, there was *much less reliance on governmental currency* than there is now. People exchanged services and goods through a variety of barter systems. In our own time, there is a trend back to this practice—but so far it's almost entirely underground, and the large majority of Americans don't really understand how it works or how they can benefit from it.

In earlier days, when a family managed to generate a surplus of money, they often tended to *invest that extra cash in something solid, some tangible property* that they could touch, feel or use.

At the present time, however, many people go directly

to banks, to the stock market, to government bonds or treasury bills, or to other forms of investment that are what might be called "intangible," because all the owner receives is a passbook or certificate which serves as evidence of the property he owns.

So these were some characteristics of the original American economy, the system of personal finances and business that existed above ground as the normative way of conducting one's daily affairs. But it's obvious that times have changed. Each of these features of our early economic system has become the exception rather than the rule. In fact, most of these first economic practices have disappeared almost completely from our visible economic network. Where they exist at all, they are carried on out of sight of the average citizen and the prying eyes of the government.

We need to recapture these early American principles and practices—but not out of nostalgia for a long-past "golden age." There is no returning to the past. But there are some basic economic truths that our forebears discovered and profited from—truths that people of any era can find helpful. It's to those truths, which today reside in the underground economy, that we'll now turn.

First, some basic definitions pertaining to the underground economy: The legal underground economy is a comprehensive but subtle network of personal financial opportunities and methods which can help both to save on current expenses and to provide security in difficult times.

It's only the *legal* underground economy that I advocate getting into. No plan based on deceit and fraud, as the illegal underground economy is, will ever yield peace and security. The *illegal underground economy* exists primarily to evade taxes and is nothing less than thievery. This

44

is a good point in our discussion to consider this outlaw network so that we can draw a clear line between the two systems.

Like its legal counterpart, the illegal underground economy evolved in an effort to recapture the freedom and independence that characterized our earliest economic system. But behind the illegal underground economy there is also a deep-rooted dishonesty that manifests itself by hiding taxable income from the government.

The resentment of oppressive taxation, together with the ease of deception, has led many to rationalize cheating on taxes through such schemes as operating a business largely on a "tax-free" cash basis. With this particular "cash business" method, much of the income passes from buyer to seller tax-free, in the sense it's never reported as income to the government.

The birth of the onerous income tax system earlier in this century really gave birth to the illegal underground economy. It's important to understand that for the most part this system consists of legitimate businesses which are run in a way designed to circumvent taxes.

There is an entirely separate network of illegal business run by organized crime, such as loan-sharking and book-making operations. These also contribute significantly to the burgeoning underground economy, but they are not the subject of this discussion. What's now of concern to us are those fundamentally legal ventures that the average person might be tempted to manipulate illegally in an effort to reduce operating costs.

This part of the illegal underground economy usually emerges through a legal small business, such as a plumbing shop. A typical business may have a fixed, government-caused overhead of 25 percent to 50 percent of total

45

business income from such things as reporting regulations, income tax levies, FICA requirements and sales taxes. This means that for every $100 that comes in to the business, between $25 and $50 is redistributed to government-related overhead. If the business's income can be hidden, however, this cost is effectively eliminated. Allow me to illustrate:

Suppose your furnace goes out, and after estimating the costs, the heating man says, "I can fix your furnace for either four hundred or two hundred dollars." Obviously, you would ask him, "What's the difference?"

"Simple," he says. "It's four hundred if I have to report it to the government or two hundred if you give me cash and I don't. And after all, why should you have to pay the government to have me fix your furnace?"

If you go along, you become part of the illegal underground economy. Take my advice and stay out of it.

I've experienced this in operation, as you perhaps also have. On one occasion, it was a heating and plumbing contractor who by law was required to buy various licenses in every city and county where he carried on business. To do so would have cost him about $12,000 a year. In addition, he was liable for the other usual state and federal contributions and taxes, such as unemployment compensation, FICA and federal income tax. These combined costs would have added more than 50 percent to his total overhead, so he chose to do the majority of this business in unreported cash. As a result, his customers got a substantial discount on the cost of his services. Unfortunately for this individual, one of his prospective customers reported him to the authorities and he's now doing contract labor for the government—as an inmate.

The ingenuity of some people in trying to beat the government out of taxes can at times seem limitless. In one of our own properties, we were in need of a sewer line hookup, and so we asked several contractors for estimates. One enterprising fellow refused to submit a written bid, but orally he quoted the job at 40 percent less than any other contractor. The catch was, he had to be paid in cash, and no receipts.

Of course we refused, but the experience was instructive because it showed me in a very personal way how common the illegal underground economy really is, and how tempting it can be. It involves a vast number of people who otherwise consider themselves honest citizens. But the visible facade of honesty may be a veneer that conceals the real action that is going on inside. The sad thing is that they have slipped into a subtle, easy-to-rationalize form of larceny that may not only get them into trouble with the law but also have the insidious effect of paving the way to other forms of illegality. It's only a small step to move from stealing from the government to stealing from an individual person if the need arises.

There have been various estimates of just how much money is involved in this illegal economy each year. The lowest estimates run around $150 billion to $250 billion— and some estimates go as high as $700 billion. If this top figure is correct, then, as one recent *Wall Street Journal* article pointed out, that would mean the underground economy may generate an income equal to more than a quarter of our gross national product.

The implications of such figures are monumental. For one thing, if you take the illegal underground economy into account, our real growth rate in the United States, as of this writing, may be 5 percent to 6 percent, rather than the 2 percent to 3 percent that the government reports.

Also, with such a strong underground economy undergirding us, a complete economic collapse would seem much less likely than if official national economic figures are accepted as accurate. (But note: We're talking here now about an *economic* collapse, not a currency collapse which focuses only on the strength of our money. A currency collapse may lead to a complete economic collapse but it doesn't necessarily have to.)

Another startling conclusion that can be drawn about the possibly gargantuan size of the illegal underground economy is the most obvious one: The government loses an incredible amount of money in unpaid taxes each year! If we could somehow get the majority of those in the illegal underground economy back into the legitimate economy, our tax revenues would grow substantially, and we could reduce the overall tax burden on the rest of us.

Here are a few more examples of how this illegal underground operates:

• Waiters and waitresses often take in almost all their money through cash tips and frequently don't report what they earn. Since it's next to impossible for the IRS to keep track of these transactions, the tax people have designed a profile of the typical waiter or waitress and their incomes. Estimates of income tax are based on these models unless the taxpayer can prove otherwise.

• A similar approach has been taken by the IRS with coin machine operators, who also deal only in cash. They are required to pay taxes based on certain guidelines set up by the IRS.

• Honorariums given to businessmen, members of the clergy and others for speaking engagements and other services often don't get reported as income on tax returns. I know because I've counseled many people who have overlooked these payments.

• One of the biggest areas of the illegal underground economy seems at first glance to be one of the most innocent—flea markets and garage sales. Yet hundreds and even thousands of taxable dollars exchange hands during these events, and I doubt if 1 percent of the transactions are reported to the IRS.

• Small retail stores sometimes alternate use of the cash registers for legal and illegal transactions. When a customer pays for an item, the proprietor, rather than registering the transaction through the cash register, opens the drawer by hitting the no-sale key. He then gives change out of the cash drawer, but the transaction is never recorded on the tape inside the register.

For example, I once bought some shaving equipment for $7 and gave the seller a ten-dollar bill for the items. He punched the cash drawer open, put my $10 into the drawer and gave me the change—but without giving me a receipt for my purchase. As far as the world or the IRS was concerned, then, my purchase never occurred. Apparently, the owner pocketed my $7 as tax-free income.

• Small jobs done by yard men, domestic workers and babysitters often result in cash payments. If you employ domestic workers and pay them more than $50 a quarter, you're supposed to file a Social Security tax form and give them a W-2 form at the end of the year. But many families just don't bother and thus contribute to the burgeoning illegal underground economy.

This dishonesty helps weaken our entire economic

system. Those who choose to be honest are penalized because they have to pay heavier taxes to fill the vacuum left by those who are evading the IRS. And those who are borderline honest often get pushed over the edge and decide to become petty thieves "like everybody else" in order to survive in our age of high inflation and taxes. It's ironic that it's the completely honest person, the one who is trying hard to do what's right, who has the most trouble operating effectively in our above-ground economy.

So what can the honest person do to fight this trend toward cheating the government, and at the same time see to his own economic survival?

There are two broad courses of action. First, people who disagree with the prevalent tax evasion that's going on should attack it *directly*, in their own personal business dealings. When it is obvious that somebody is offering you an illegal deal, even if the price of the goods or services is far cheaper that way, don't accept it! I'm not suggesting that you go on a witch-hunt and challenge every cash transaction you encounter as being necessarily illegal. But if more honest people take a strong stand on the clear-cut cases of tax cheating, others will follow.

Realistically though, there are limits to what can be accomplished individually. So it's also necessary to take the fight to Congress in an effort to make the system more equitable for the honest taxpayer.

What sort of measure might do the job? A radical but fair solution would change things for the better almost immediately: We should establish a 10 percent tax rate for *everybody* and allow no deductions or alterations of that percentage, no matter what the income level. Then, with this drastically simplified system, the federal government could eliminate all the complicated IRS regulations, the attendant legal staffs and other bureaucrats. The government could then marshal all its resources to impose heavy penalties on those who still refused to comply with the new, relatively light 10 percent rate.

With this program in effect, the rate of compliance would rise dramatically as the tax evaders saw they had much more to lose than to gain by sticking to their cash-only transactions. In addition, the federal government would take in at least as much money with this simple across-the-board 10 percent rate as it does with the complex progressive tax structure that now exists. Finally, the illegal underground economy would most likely shrink down to those hard-core thieves who steal as a way of life.

Crusades against the tax structure may appeal to you as part of a long-term solution to the burdens imposed on honest people by the illegal underground economy. But what steps can you take *right now* to ease your personal economic burdens and at the same time stay within the boundaries of the law?

The answer to this question is simple: Resolve to recapture some of the basic economic principles on which the success of our American system is based by entering the *legal* underground economy. Then you can begin to enjoy benefits that will far exceed anything you'll pick up by concocting elaborate tax evasion schemes, and you'll sleep a lot better at night as well.

Here are the main "entrances" to this legal underground economy and some indications about what we'll say about them in the rest of the book:

Entrance 1: Develop an Emergency Store of Food and Household Products. Just as the more prudent early Americans always prepared for the worst so that they could be sure they would at least survive during especially hard times, you also should stock up on staple goods. This will put you in a stronger position as a current consumer and prepare you to withstand any temporary social disruption that might accompany a currency collapse. But this does *not* mean you should hoard food—only store a reasonable amount.

Entrance 2: Get into an Economic Support Community. Perhaps the most significant part of the underground economy is the network of voluntary associations, churches and other close-knit groups that have sprung up in our nation since its founding. These associations are truly "nations within the nation," though some still lie dormant. But if the spiritual and emotional motivations are there, these groups can be mobilized as a powerful undergirding for your individual efforts to survive and thrive in a period of economic trouble.

Our focus in discussing these groups will be on ways to reinforce economic self-help and mutual sharing through such arrangements as a "moneyless credit network" and barter systems.

Entrance 3: Plug into the Alternative Job Market. It's important to develop an entrepreneurial, self-employed base which you can fall back on in the event you lose your job. One of the strengths of our ancestors was that they often set up their own businesses and worked for themselves. There was a direct correlation between their own level of hard work and expertise and the amount of money they made. Similarly, in today's underground economy, one of the best forms of insurance against high unemployment and against inflation is to develop a skill which will enable you to earn money independently, at the ever-rising rates for services that prevail generally in the economy.

Entrance 4: Set Up a Crisis Budget for Your Family. A key element in the legal underground economy is organizing your personal finances so that (1) you get the most mileage out of every dollar that comes into your hands, and (2) you keep completely out of personal debt. This approach, which also characterized those with the best business heads among our forebears, will make you financially stronger and more resilient in the event of a collapse. It will also enable you to build up a surplus so that you can invest in crisis-proof investments that will cushion you still further in case of hard times.

Entrance 5: Plunge Immediately into Crisis-Proof Investments. In this section of the book, we'll define just what the good investments are for those involved in the underground economy and how individuals at different income levels should get into them. As I evaluated the various possible investments to get into at the present time, I discovered some interesting similarities between my own conclusions and the conclusions by successful American business people in the heyday of our entrepreneurial spirit a century or more ago.

This, then, is an introduction to the five entrances to the legal underground economy. Now let's move quickly ahead and begin to explore this subterranean network in depth—and find some ways you can improve your personal financial position dramatically.

CHAPTER FIVE

The Underground Pantry Principle

Many of the early American settlers were obsessed with the idea of survival—and for good reason.

Those who started out with an uncleared tract of virgin land knew that, despite the hostile elements and unpredictable Indian tribes in the vicinity, they had to grow enough food by year's end to make it through the winter. So it was quite appropriate that many of these pioneers were called "subsistence farmers." In other words, if they could only subsist through another year and win the battle against starvation, they were winners.

Our society has come a long way since those days. Yet I'm not sure we haven't lost something important. In our era, for the first time in the history of mankind, a substantial majority of an entire nation—the American people— have come to *expect* someone else to supply them with everything, every day.

Solomon, whose sayings were well-known to our American forebears, described the sensible plan they often used for storing some abundance in good times in anticipation of lean years:

> *Go to the ant, you sluggard;*
> *consider its ways and be wise!*
> *It has no commander,*
> *no overseer or ruler,*
> *yet it stores its provisions in summer*
> *and gathers its food at harvest.*
> *How long will you lie there, you sluggard?*
> *When will you get up from your sleep?*
>
> PROVERBS 6:6–10,
> New International Version

Somehow, we believe that our technology has eliminated any possibility that we might actually go hungry. So did the people of the Roman Empire, until their affluence made them lazy and soft—and they found themselves totally unprepared for national crises.

But some preparation for a possible crisis is prudent and wise. It's *not* an inevitable law of economics that Americans must always enjoy the good life. In fact, if you look at the entire sweep of human history, you'll see that we exist in an economic oasis. And, as we've seen in previous chapters, there's a good likelihood that in the near future we may experience a profound economic down cycle.

We need balance in planning, not extremism. For example, some pessimistic economic forecasters believe it's smart to store one year's supply of food to ensure survival. I don't agree with that advice for a couple of reasons.

THE UNDERGROUND PANTRY PRINCIPLE

First of all, such a plan will work for only a very few people and breeds an attitude of distrust in our society. So having a hoard of dehydrated food—or even a well-stocked pantry filled with crates upon crates of tuna fish and canned vegetables—is not going to be the answer, at least not for most of us.

Imagine the situation in a city if residents actually had to go through even a few *months* when they couldn't buy anything from the local grocer. With large numbers of starving people on the streets, our society would be in a state of total chaos and probably well on the way toward a major revolution. As a matter of fact, if we face that sort of crisis, I would strongly advise you to *forget* any food you've stored at home and head for the hills without further delay and start eating grubs if necessary. Why? Because your very life will probably be in danger from marauding mobs that are roaming about your neighborhood looking for whatever supplies they can find. At this point, the extreme security advocates would suggest you also have a mountain retreat stocked with food and guns, just in case.

Secondly, such a plan runs contrary to my belief that we care for others in need. Many of those who hoard rationalize it by saying they *want* to be able to help others later. But in truth, if they aren't helping now, they won't later, either.

So as an alternative, I'd suggest you try following the *Underground Pantry Principle*. Under this approach you store up three months' worth of food and staple supplies. These are normal grocery items that you customarily buy. Why this amount? There are three main reasons, which, taken together, should put you in a stronger position both

57

in the present and also in any future collapse. I refer to these as the three basic parts to the Underground Pantry Principle.

Part 1. In the first place, it's a good idea to have a "buffer," in anticipation of any possible food shortage during an economic crisis. If the collapse is short-lived, you simply eat up the overage. If it's longer, you stretch out your extra supplies.

Remember: There will be a preliminary period during which a wave of economic instability begins to build. Increasing numbers of businesses go bankrupt; individual bankruptcies multiply as people lose their jobs and can't meet their credit payments; banks fail; and the hard-pressed federal government finally steps in to freeze fixed assets and revamp the monetary system.

Groceries and other supplies will begin to tighten up during this period and may eventually dry up altogether in many parts of the country during the three-to-four week peak of the crisis. For example, independent fruit and vegetable truckers operating out of the West Coast may elect to suspend their shipments to the East as economic problems worsen. The reason is obvious: Why truck goods and get paid in worthless currency? Truckers aren't altruistic; they haul food for profit. As a result, there may be a drastic shortage of food supplies that could develop in some of the large eastern cities.

Even the rumor of this happening will cause panic in the cities and fear-stricken citizens will strip the shelves of all available food. Evidence of this can be seen with the threat of a hurricane in Miami, or an ice storm in Atlanta.

The average grocery store carries only a few days' supply of food as it is. If you walk into the normal supermarket in Miami on the day before a hurricane, you'll find almost no food of consequence on the shelves. Or check the typical food store in Manhattan or any other big city on Sunday evening: There are huge gaps on the shelves because shoppers have stocked up for just one weekend. Now multiply these conditions by several weeks of panic over a lack of food, and you'll get some idea about the magnitude of the crisis we may be facing.

So as you can see, I think it's important to give yourself a cushion of basic foods and supplies to ensure that you'll make it comfortably over the violent hump of any currency crisis. But this is not the only element in the Underground Pantry Principle.

Part 2. Another reason for setting a goal of three months' worth of food on your shelves is that you may be able to help others who get caught short of basic supplies during a crisis.

Now, you may scoff openly and think, "It's every man for himself if we run out of food!" Or you may just be bored with this point because you think I'm throwing in an obligatory exhortation to altruism. But actually, if you take either of these positions, you'd totally miss my point. For by planning to help others, you'll be contributing to an atmosphere of mutual aid that will work to your own benefit as well.

To put it another way, think about your decision to help others as an *investment* of your time and energies in the larger community. But unlike many of the investments you may try on the stock market, this community investment is one on which you can't lose. There's a guarantee, which stems from a basic spiritual principle, that when you give to others, you'll eventually get something valuable in return. We'll explore this concept more at a later point. For now, let's move on to the third element in the Underground Pantry Principle.

Part 3. The first two parts to the Underground Pantry Principle relate to the impending currency collapse. But the third aspect has a more immediate application to your personal finances in the here and now.

It is important that a three-month stock of food and other basic supplies be kept on hand so that major food shopping can be done primarily during sales and growing seasons, when food items are lower in cost.

Probably most families will have to stock up on these extra canned goods, dry cereals and other such things over a period of time—perhaps even a year—because they don't have enough surplus money to purchase the extra food in large quantities all at once. But if you begin a systematic program right now, you'll have a comfortable store of extra items in a few months. And then, with your Underground Pantry in shape, you can embark on a systematic approach to buying low-priced foods on sale.

You may well find you can go for several weeks without purchasing any staple items at all because your local grocery stores aren't offering the sales you seek. But you cannot afford to wait to build up these stores! If apathy sets in, you may find yourself facing a bare cupboard and no choices.

How low should you allow your Underground Pantry to get before you begin to build it up again using the cyclical shopping system we've just discussed?

Since three months is the average amount of goods to keep on hand, a good rule of thumb for a minimum would be about one month. Obviously, if you're bargain shopping, not all items will be purchased at one time, and if one product is low, another will likely be at maximum. If worse comes to worst, you might have to eat a lot of one item for a while!

Now, here's one final point about this Underground Pantry Principle before we move on. You may be wondering exactly what items you should buy to build up your pantry to this three-month maximum supply.

There is no "typical shopping list," but there are some general guidelines you should follow in making your purchases. First of all, avoid the freeze-dried or dehydrated foods because the costs are usually excessive. Also, if you buy food supplies this way, then you eliminate any possibility of using the sales-shopping concept we discussed. The concept is based on the premise of accumulating and replacing normal foodstuffs regularly. That would be rather hard to do with dehydrated food—because I doubt that anyone in your family would be satisfied with a bowl of dehydrated meat, even on special occasions!

So the items you buy should be ordinary foods that you can use at your daily meals—but foods which will keep for long periods on your shelf. Obviously, this requirement limits you mostly to things like canned foods, powdered milk and the like. For example, if you happen to like tuna fish and find that your family can get along on one can a week, then you would buy four to five cans for each month, or a maximum of fifteen cans for your Underground Pantry.

You may also want to consider stocking up on perishables, like fresh meats, which you can freeze. But usually this will be limited to fresh vegetables and fruits which can be purchased during growing seasons and then canned.

By now, you should have a fairly good idea of the Underground Pantry Principle. The heart of this concept, as with all the other aspects of the underground economy, is that it involves a move back to some of the fundamental principles that gave our forefathers economic power and security. They were pragmatic about their need to be responsible for as much of their own security as possible. We need a modification of their philosophy to fit our modern system of retailing.

But even if you agree with the basic idea of acquiring an emergency food supply and using it to do sales shopping, you may still conclude, "No matter how diligently we prepare, our family may still be caught short of food and other supplies during a big economic crisis. But several families working together and agreeing to share work and goods with one another could provide much more comprehensive security for everybody."

That kind of reasoning leads naturally to the subject of group food purchasing and other community exchange and cooperative projects. We're next going to discuss in detail why it's an excellent idea to start getting involved right now in food co-ops, barter systems, clothes-swapping arrangements and similar programs. These things represent the heart of the underground economy and have the potential for saving tremendous amounts of money—while helping you avoid much of the hyperinflation of the retail supply system.

But because of the great tax-avoiding potential inherent in this underground exchange system—and especially in the noncash barter area—the Internal Revenue Service is always on the lookout for ways to extend its regulatory control over cooperative ventures. So let's first take a look at your responsibilities to the government as you begin to get involved in noncash transactions with other participants in the underground economy.

CHAPTER SIX

The Underground Exchange System

Good businessmen know that if they try to operate only in the traditional, open economic arena, where the federal government regulates and taxes every transaction, their profits will be reduced or eliminated.

But fortunately, the American economy is still free enough to offer channels in which the knowledgeable entrepreneur can sidestep the system and legally reduce or eliminate much of the burdensome taxation. The informed person can not only survive but also build a sizable fortune if he or she knows how to use tax-free exchanges and low-tax barter trades. These represent the essence of the free-market system that made our economy strong.

As we've seen, there are illegal ways to beat the government in the underground economy, mainly through the use of cash transactions to evade the payment of taxes. And the sense of unfairness, which has tainted the attitude of much of the American population as a result of burdensome government regulation and taxation, has pushed many into this outlaw realm—to the tune of billions of dollars a year. In fact, as has been mentioned, the amount of money involved in this mass cash-economy tax evasion may run as high as $700 billion, or more than one fourth of our gross national product.

But it's important to distinguish between tax *evasion*, which is illegal, and tax *avoidance*, which is perfectly legal and desirable. You evade taxes, and may be opening yourself up to criminal penalties, if you fail to file an income tax return or intentionally declare less income than you actually earn. But there are also many legal ways to use the law, or just step outside its scope to avoid the payment of excessive taxes, and that's one of the things I want to stress in this chapter.

For example, many sophisticated investors who are in a high income tax bracket may put their money into "tax shelters" that enable their investments to grow, but without the necessity of paying the highest tax rates on any increases. Some real estate investments, which we'll be discussing in detail later in this book, fall into this category. The reason the well-to-do are attracted to these deals is that the deductions for interest payments, depreciation on buildings, taxes and other such costs may equal or exceed any income the investor earns. And that will mean he doesn't owe any taxes—even though he may, quite legally, pocket a huge return.

But I'm getting ahead of myself in discussing the investment aspect of the underground economy. Before we get into that, there are other, extremely lucrative and entirely legal ways that you can gain monetary benefits that are taxable at a much reduced rate. And the crown jewel of these cashless techniques is the contemporary version of that ancient system of exchange known as *barter*, which goes back to the earliest periods of our existence and was in full bloom during our nation's formation.

In many sections of colonial America, where currency was not widely available, our ancestors got used to carrying on their business transactions by exchanging goods and services instead of money. This method of doing business could be cumbersome and inexact since nobody was ever quite sure just how many bales of hay or cotton it took to make an equal exchange for a good horse or wagon. And because it was more convenient to carry paper currency than some farm commodity in their purse or hip pocket, most people were quite happy to make the shift over to money when the federal government got stronger and was able to control the nation's monetary system.

But what the average citizen didn't foresee was just how controlling the federal government could become in overseeing money transactions. As the government's needs increased in this century, the tax rates also increased to give the federal bureaucracy a means of paying for its programs. And when these tax rates finally became confiscatory—especially in the 1920's and thereafter—more and more individuals began to return to various forms of the old barter system to avoid the grasp of the Internal Revenue Service.

In other words, Americans began to *go underground*, both legally and illegally, to avoid taxes. It's ironic that a movement has begun to return to those economic roots that we once so freely gave up. But that's exactly what has happened, as increasing numbers of astute business

67

experts, in an effort to escape government control and strangulation, have looked for and found ways to conduct their dealings completely outside normal channels.

Let me give you a couple of examples of how this sort of thing is being done on a rather large scale, and then we'll examine how you can take advantage of the technique yourself.

A barter system can be defined simply as an arrangement for the swapping of goods or services, without using any medium of exchange like money. You can see the big advantage of this way of doing business if we really are headed for a currency collapse because, if a good part of your business is conducted *without* money, you don't have to worry so much about what may happen to the money.

But big corporations are interested in barter exchanges for reasons other than protection against a monetary crisis. For one thing, by setting up elaborate systems to trade goods and services, they can reduce the need for accumulating huge cash reserves to purchase expensive equipment—and they stay ahead of the game even if they have to pay taxes on the exchanges after they occur.

Let me explain by giving you a couple of concrete examples. There are about six or seven very large computer-controlled corporate barter systems in this country that do a multimillion dollar business each year.

One way they operate is for the barter exchange itself to go out and purchase equipment and then offer it to member corporations in exchange for other equipment. The central barter organization makes its profit by arranging the property exchanges at a higher price than they paid for the equipment and then pocketing the difference in dollars, or *barter credits*.

But the most common way for these big barter organizations to function is strictly as a broker for equipment that corporations already own. For example, suppose some company in Atlanta needs a piece of $500 typesetting equipment, which a party in California happens to have. But the Atlanta people don't have anything they can exchange directly with the California company.

At this point, the barter outfit steps in and says they have located a third party, down in New Orleans, which has a piece of equipment that the California people would like—say a copying machine, which we'll assume has the same $500 value as the typesetting equipment.

So now the stage is set for the barter exchange: The company in California agrees to ship the typesetting equipment to the Atlanta company, and as a result the Atlanta company would be debited 500 credits and the California company would get 500 barter credits. Then, the California group uses their 500 credits to get the copying machine from the New Orleans company.

The final result of this particular transaction is that the Atlanta company still owes somebody in the barter system 500 credits worth of equipment, the California company is even, and the New Orleans organization has the right to 500 credits worth of goods from someone. Usually, there is a requirement that those with a deficit of barter credits must pay off their debt in *usable* equipment or money within a *limited period of time.*

The barter swaps are quite simple if the equipment is of equal value, but of course, that's rarely the case. Experts must first assess exactly what a piece of used equipment is worth, and a certain number of barter credits are assigned to it. The barter exchange always marks up each item by a number of points and takes those extra points as payment for brokerage. Then, when the equipment gets out into the system and transactions start taking place, barter credits get added and subtracted from the accounts of different members of the system. The central barter organization can also participate in these deals by trading its brokerage credits for equipment, which it may in turn sell on the open market.

One of the largest systems of barter exchanges ever set up involved military aircraft. In one series of deals, the fellow in charge of this exchange heard that the Mexican government was in the process of phasing out all its old DC 3's. He also learned that another government in South America wanted some of those planes, so he arranged a swap—but the second government didn't have enough money to pay for the planes. They did have a lot of bananas, though.

Unfortunately, the Mexican government didn't want bananas. They wanted airplane tires. So the barter man started looking around in other parts of the world for some substitute barter items. Finally, he discovered a country in the Middle East that was willing to trade some oil for the bananas; another country had some rugs they wanted to swap for the oil; and still another country was ready to make a deal for the rugs in exchange for some airplane tires they had on hand.

So through this series of complex international deals, the barter man was able to consummate the transaction between the Mexican government with the airplanes and the South American regime with the surplus of bananas. And he also made a profit on each of the intermediate deals he set up by marking up the trade value of each set of items and then selling what he had left over after each deal on the open market.

Both of these examples of big business barters involve potentially taxable transactions, but the individuals and companies involved in them can still often come out far ahead financially—and may end up paying little or no tax. For example, those involved in a barter exchange can mark off the cost of the item they are trading, just as they would mark off the cost of an ordinary item they sold for currency. In other words, if someone trades a copying machine that cost $500 for a typewriter that cost $500, each party could deduct the "cost basis" of his respective property, which in each case would be $500. And because neither party would have realized any taxable income in this case, neither would owe any income tax.

On the other hand, the central barter exchange—and the barter man, in the case of the military aircraft—would owe tax on what they had earned as brokerage fees or credits. And any member company of an American barter system would owe tax on the *barter credits* they received, in lieu of property.

Now, these are big barter exchange deals that involve a lot of expensive property and high finance. But you can get involved in exactly the same sort of thing on a much smaller scale—and end up far ahead of the game in your personal finances.

Remember: The barter system started off in a small way in the American colonies, where the key factor was that individuals in different fields started generating a surplus of goods. The farmer might harvest more wheat than he could use in a given year. And the shoemaker, by working a little longer each day, might put out more shoes than he could easily sell. So those with such surpluses started getting together and trading the extra goods they had accumulated.

In our own time, the simplest barter exchange you can get involved in is to walk across your backyard and agree to exchange the use of your lawnmower for your neighbor's chain saw. Or you might decide to baby-sit for his kids this weekend if he'll mow your lawn while you're away on vacation.

Many times, assistance like this may be offered just because people are friends and they want to volunteer to help each other out, without expecting anything in return. But sometimes neighbors get involved in more formal exchanges of goods and services—especially when the agreed-upon tasks become regular, time-consuming things. And those transactions are nothing more than barters conducted on the lowest, grass-roots levels of our society.

What are the legal and tax implications of these barter arrangements?

As increasing numbers of people get involved in exchanges of goods and services, which take place largely outside the regulation of the federal bureaucracy, you can bet the government isn't sleeping. Tax dollars are at stake, and that's a serious matter in these times, when the federal and local governments are hard-pressed for funds to cover programs that are being threatened through the high cost of inflation and also the conservative movement to limit government spending.

At this point, the law is in a state of flux on the barter issue. The IRS is pushing hard for increasing its power to collect taxes on barters, and private tax experts are countering that the IRS is going too far and would lose in tax

court on some of its positions. But even with this confu-
sion, it's important to lay the issues out on the table right
now because much of what I'm going to say about the
advantages of community support systems hinges on the
extent to which those systems can exist largely outside
the realm of government control.

Many tax attorneys questioned on which barter transactions between individuals they absolutely feel are taxable replied that *only exchanges of those goods and
services which you offer for pay in your business are taxable.* In other words, if an owner of a television store
swaps a TV to the owner of a furniture store in return
for a couch, that's definitely a taxable exchange. The tax,
as was the case with the big-business barters we talked
about, will be determined by the fair market value of
the products exchanged. And those involved in the barter
will be able to subtract from that fair market value the
cost basis—or the amount they originally paid—for the
item they are giving up.

Similarly, these private tax experts say, if a doctor ren-
ders some medical service to an attorney in return for
having a will drawn up, that's a taxable exchange of services, and each person has to declare on his income tax
return the equivalent monetary value of the services he
received. So, if the medical services were worth $100 and
the will would have cost $100, each individual must
include an extra $100 in income tax on his return.

But most private tax lawyers and accountants came to a
different conclusion on the situation where the individuals
are exchanging goods and services which are *not* part of
their regular income-producing business pursuits or part
of a "professional" barter exchange.

For example, if an attorney who is a woodworking hobbyist makes a table for a doctor who is an auto-repair buff, and the doctor in exchange gives the lawyer a valve job, the tax experts agree that this transaction should not be taxable.

But the IRS disagrees. They regard *any* exchange of goods and services between two individuals, for which value is received on both sides, to be a taxable exchange. In fact, the IRS is so concerned about the growing underground economy in barter transactions that they have rendered a couple of revenue rules on this subject.

One of these rulings relates to what the IRS calls *barter club transactions,* and the service states its position this way: "A barter club uses credit units to credit or debit members' accounts for goods or services provided or received. As soon as units are credited to the member's account, the member may use them to purchase goods or services or may sell or transfer the units to other members. The value of credit units received is includible in the gross income of members for the taxable year in which the units are credited to their accounts. The dollar value of units received for services by an employee of the club, who may use the units in the same manner as other members, is includible in gross income for the taxable year in which received." (Rev. Rul. 80–52. 1980).

In a recent U.S. district court decision, the IRS even won the right to get a barter club's member lists and records of transactions.

In the other ruling, which concerns the *exchange by professionals of their regular business services,* the IRS said, ". . . the owner of an apartment building who receives a work of art created by a professional artist in return for the rent-free use of an apartment must include in income the fair market value of the work of art, and the artist must include the fair rental value of the apartment." (Rev. Rul. 79–24. 1979).

The interpretation given by some IRS agents on the service's position on barters goes further than either of these rulings. The first ruling related to formal barter organizations, and the second dealt mainly with the exchange of goods and services which were part of the individuals' regular occupations. But there are IRS representatives who would levy taxes in the situation where two private individuals, not in a barter organization, exchanged skills developed as hobbies.

So, as you can see, the law in this field is in a state of change and uncertainty, and you'll have to make up your own mind as to the position you'll take toward the taxability of any barter transactions you may engage in. But as the situation stands, keep these guidelines in mind:

• Experts agree that if you exchange goods or services involved in your regular business, you can be taxed on the value of what you've received.

• If you and your tax consultants decide that the IRS is all wet in its position on barter clubs or any other issue, you can take the service to court, regardless of the existence of any revenue ruling. A ruling by the service is only a formal statement of their position, but it's not law. Their position only becomes law when a Tax Court rules in their favor, and even that decision can be challenged in higher appellate courts. But if you're going to challenge the IRS, you have to be willing to put in a considerable amount of time, and probably a fair amount of money—especially if you get a lawyer to represent you rather than trying to argue your case yourself.

• You're more likely to come under the scrutiny of the IRS if you conduct your barter transactions through an established barter club than if you engage in them on a less formal basis, either as an independent individual or as part of an organization that exists primarily for some purpose other than bartering.

These, then, are a few examples and principles to introduce you to the basics of barter. Next, we'll consider in some detail how you can set up a barter system yourself. The most effective barter arrangements are often tied closely to a well-established community that can offer you much more than just barter opportunities. Above all, don't allow the IRS to bully you out of your right to exchange your goods or services for those of your friends. At worst you'll be taxed on the value received, which is still better than paying retail. Now let me take some time now to go into more detail on the kind of support community that will help you get maximum benefit from the underground exchange network.

CHAPTER SEVEN

===

Capitalizing on the Economic Self-help Network

One of the greatest traditions we have in this country is that of the voluntary association.

A major reason that many of the early settlers came to America was to escape religious and other persecutions and to be able to meet freely together to share and act on deeply held beliefs. This conviction is reflected throughout our laws and perhaps attains its ultimate expression in the First Amendment to the U.S. Constitution: "Congress shall make no law . . . abridging . . . the right of the people peaceably to assemble . . ."

Harvard Professor James Luther Adams, an internationally recognized expert on voluntary associations, traces our American tradition back to the New Testament admonition to "render unto Caesar that which is Caesar's and unto

God that which is God's." He says that as a result of this idea, the state was placed "within limits and under criticism" and the "independent religious association in no way considered itself the creature of the state."

Adams also notes that in the eighteenth and nineteenth centuries, associations sprang up to achieve every imaginable practical purpose and to right all sorts of wrongs—from penal and educational reform to women's rights. "Clearly, many of these associations have changed economic behavior," he writes.

And then Professor Adams goes on to quote from a 1911 lecture by the German economic philosopher Max Weber:

". . . America is the association-land par excellence. In America membership in some middle-class association belongs directly to one's legitimation as a gentleman . . . . Today the association furnishes the ethical qualification test for the businessman, certifying that he is worthy of credit. American democracy is no sand heap, but a maze of exclusive sects, societies and clubs. These support the selection of those adapted to American life; they support it in that they help such people to business, political and every kind of success in social life. In these associations the American learns to put himself over."

These words, which were uttered by Weber not so long ago—in the early years of this century—are still true to some extent. But all too few people these days are taking full advantage of the rights and benefits of free association which are essential to free enterprise.

In this discussion of associations the thing to keep in mind is that they are groups working together for the common good. To be effective, community associations must emulate, at least in part, the voluntary associations of our nation's earlier history—groups that were formed to *do* things and achieve important goals, and not just to attract members who sat passively, listening to a guest speaker talk about *his* (or *her*) exploits.

The closest parallel to the kind of community I'm referring to is the *koinonia* cell group—also called a fellowship or sharing community—of the early Christian church. That Greek word, *koinonia*, carries the connotation of an activist group, where the members interact constantly with one another to achieve some concrete reform or personal transformation.

The writer of the book of Hebrews perhaps put it best: "And let us consider how we may spur one another on toward love and good deeds. Let us not give up meeting together, as some are in the habit of doing, but let us encourage one another—and all the more as you see the day [of Judgment] approaching." (Heb. 10:24–25, NIV)

A local community group can function most effectively if all members share common objectives and are willing to sacrifice individual whims and wishes to achieve the benefits of group participation—benefits which include but aren't limited to financial security and savings.

For the purposes of this book, I'll assume that a significant objective of any small support community you join will be economic. Of course, it may well be that the major goal of your association will be to enhance people's spiritual lives or render a neighborhood service. Church groups, for example, develop some of the best associations for economic stabilization because many of the members share common financial goals and assumptions about sharing with others. Obviously, however, these groups have a broader primary purpose than merely conferring financial advantages on their members.

Voluntary associations may find that most distrust and

many inhibitions are absent because their members often share a common set of values and spiritual assumptions. For these groups, mutual trust and dedication to uniform standards can make it easier for them to work together on self-help projects, where each participant must demonstrate individual responsibility and submit to some form of group regulations or discipline.

Some of the projects that you can participate in with a small economic support group include (1) cooperative buying of food at much lower prices than you can get as an individual shopper; (2) sharing of tools and other household equipment; (3) pooling of clothing, especially among families with growing kids; (4) developing barter systems to exchange goods without having to use your hard-earned cash; and (5) swapping necessary skills, which you and your community members possess, to avoid paying inflated service charges to outside businesses.

This community association concept is absolutely essential for survival during any financial collapse, and it dovetails with some of the other underground economy concepts we'll discuss throughout this book. For example, if you're having trouble trimming your expenses to fit into a budget plan, one method to ease the financial strain is to reduce the cost of food and clothing through some sort of cooperative buying or swapping program.

Also, if and when the economic disaster strikes, you'll find that involvement in a community cooperative may well mean the difference between eating or not eating—or at least not eating very well. In other words, if you lose your job during the crisis or otherwise face personal financial difficulties, you won't have to go it alone. You can expect to be helped by other members of your group—

and you may also be in a position to render aid to others who may face tougher times than you.

To repeat: *The foundation of any community cooperative must be a commonly shared value system.* In addition, the ultimate objective should be to help others as well as yourself. Otherwise, selfishness and self-preservation take over and will destroy the usefulness of any community effort. In my experience, the greatest resource available to make such a group function effectively is to build the group on a deep-rooted religious faith. But the spiritual commitment of each member must be genuine and not mere lip service. Otherwise, the participants won't really be sharing the same values, and it may well be impossible for them to settle on a common set of objectives.

Also, when the community cooperative is part of a larger group, such as a church, the additional resources of that umbrella group will be available if needed. By supporting your local church with at least 10 percent of your income, you are in essence planting seeds for the future.

Those *koinonia* fellowship groups mentioned earlier had important economic as well as spiritual dimensions, because the members of the early house churches held all things in common. They ate their meals together and supported other groups that were undergoing greater hardships. Thus, when one group ran into economic difficulties —as the branch of the church in Jerusalem did in the first century—then the Apostle Paul called on the believers at Corinth to send some money from their abundance to help out.

Our American forefathers also believed in pitching in and helping out their neighbors, both with physical effort and also with money. They possessed a community spirit that led them to support one another economically as a matter of course. To neglect or refuse to respond to a neighbor's misfortune was unthinkable. People weren't islands, and families weren't isolated units. Community relationships and responsibilities were as important as individual rights and integrity. And anybody who tried to go it alone was more often than not regarded as a misfit. You see, those early American settlers knew that their very survival depended on how well they worked together and how solidly they could count on one another in a crisis.

Unfortunately, we've lost this strong sense of community ties. And we've lost the economic as well as the personal and spiritual benefits that can go along with it. But the crucial concept of the support community hasn't disappeared entirely. It's still alive and well today in the underground economy. What follows is a suggested plan of action for your own personal participation in this community concept.

First, get involved in a local church whose members accept active responsibility for each other spiritually and materially and are willing to offer mutual aid every day of the week. They view themselves, literally, as physical members—like hands and toes—of one complete and harmonious body.

Obviously, if you are not religious, you may not be drawn to a house of worship. But the basic principles, such as finding a group with common values and objectives, are still important, so you'll have to try to find some other community service group that comes close to what is being described.

So getting involved in a group means more than just attending meetings or occasional worship services. It means taking an active role in helping to establish food co-ops, service bulletins or religious education programs. The more programs you participate in, the better you'll get to know the organization and especially the people in it. You'll begin to understand their strengths and weaknesses in working with others and also the level of their commitment to basic spiritual and family values.

It's necessary to understand the nature of the people in your chosen organization if you hope to approach some of them about starting an economic support group. Why? Because a mutual-aid community of the type we're talking about will quickly fall apart if the wrong people, with widely divergent expectations, get thrown together.

I should include one qualification here, though, just so you won't get the wrong impression: I'm not suggesting that you join a church or any other organization with the *sole* intention of using it as a base to form an economic community that will make you secure in a currency crisis or any other economic difficulty. But it's important and perfectly proper in any organization to develop a community foundation that can reduce costs and also respond in times of crisis.

So now you're in a community service organization. But what is the next step?

The very next step is to commit not only your time but also your finances to your organization which is involved in helping to expand the community concept. Now, to what extent should you contribute financial support to your chosen group?

Some people I counsel balk at beginning with a tithe, or 10 percent, of their gross income, especially if they haven't previously made this commitment. I encourage them (and you) to pick *some* amount and begin to share with others.

83

Unless you and others like you are willing to sacrifice a little, there is no way this community concept can work. The current attitude of "let someone else do it" is a root cause of many of our economic problems.

As you get more deeply involved in your community, you'll find others who feel similarly and are willing to act accordingly.

Now let's move on to the specifics of an economic support program. Here are four possible ways you can band together with like-minded people in the underground economy to cut your costs, ease the pressure on your budget and build a needed surplus.

The Food Cooperative. In a few years food prices will escalate to the point where the cost of oil will seem cheap in comparison. I believe it's wise to set aside about 15 percent of net income for food. But that percentage is only appropriate at today's prices. It's possible that food prices will go so high that they will replace home costs as the most expensive item in the average family budget.

There will be a number of important factors that will influence food costs. First, a major component of food production is fertilizer, which is made in part from petroleum. Secondly, many small farmers are steadily going out of business, and ultimately only a few large cooperatives will dominate the agricultural industry. With less competition, there will be less pressure to keep prices low.

So the average family will have no alternative but to pay the prices that the corporate planners prescribe. One of the factors that helped many people survive in the Great Depression of the 1930's was that 80 percent of Americans lived on farms and were able to grow much of their own food. Supermarkets were an experiment then, whereas now they are a necessity. But today, nearly 80 percent of all Americans live in cities and do not try to grow their own food. They are totally dependent on the outside supply system every single day.

You can develop a cushion against the impact of rising prices or an economic crisis by maintaining a minimum supply through an Underground Pantry, as we've suggested in an earlier chapter, and shopping only during sales and growing seasons. But in the long run, everyone will be affected by the food price increases.

Ultimately, it will become increasingly critical for the average family to participate in some type of food cooperative. A food co-op is a small group of compatible people of basically the same general tastes and income level, who band together to buy food in bulk, at wholesale prices. The savings are passed on to the members, who supply the labor. A well-run group can cut 15 percent to 25 percent off their retail grocery bill costs. Many people have unrealistic expectations of saving 40 percent or more by joining one of these organizations, but this is rarely if ever possible.

The ideal size for a food co-op is about eight to ten families. A group should not go over ten because of problems with storage and transport of the food. But if the number drops below eight, then you lose many of the economies of size and the ability to buy items in bulk quantities. The best way to locate candidates for your co-op is to post a notice on the bulletin board of your church or other service organization asking those interested in joining a food-buying co-op to contact you. In most cases, you'll be swamped with interested inquirers—probably many more than the maximum of ten families you need. So it will probably be necessary to pare down the candidates to the most effective group.

Any productive co-op, which involves the joint spending of money, should be controlled by a definite set of rules which every member must follow. This requirement will become the most important element in your final selection process.

First, the people in the group must be relatively compatible in life-style. I know one co-op that consists mostly of airline pilots and their families who make $70,000 to $100,000 a year. It probably wouldn't work very well to include a factory worker who makes $18,000. The kinds of food and other consumer items that would appeal to people on such widely divergent income levels are usually so different that the families just couldn't sustain a long-term economic relationship—that is, not unless the pilots decided to live on $18,000 a year.

It would probably also be unwise to try to match couples who have young children with childless couples because the needs of the two groups are too unlike. Similarly, a basic conflict might arise by matching a meat-and-potatoes person with a health-food enthusiast. One generally wants red meat a couple of times a week, and the other might desire large orders of wheat germ and tiger's milk. It's possible, of course, that people with different interests can teach and learn from one another, so some variations may add a little spice to the personal relationships in the community. But too wide a gulf in economic tastes and values will probably do more harm than good.

Finally, the members of your co-op should live fairly

close together. Usually, people should not try to band together unless they live within about fifteen minutes, or ten miles, of one another. Remember: Part of the advantage of being in a co-op is the opportunity to save a good sum of money in a *reasonable* amount of time. But if you must travel long distances to pick up or deliver food, it's probably not going to be worth your while to participate.

So it's important to make a commonsense evaluation of the candidates for your food co-op just to be certain that, on the surface, they appear compatible in as many ways as possible. A brief but thorough questionnaire will aid in doing this. Once you've selected a few candidates through this sort of brief examination, the next step is to schedule a meeting to discuss the particulars of the co-op concept. At that time, a more detailed questionnaire should be distributed to help assess such points as various skills available within the group, the family size of each participant and available vehicles for food pickup and delivery.

Selecting people who are close to one another in personal interests and living styles is important if you ever want to move beyond food purchases to other cooperative areas—such as a job-skill bank where different members exchange services with one another, or the sharing of recreation facilities.

Finally, when you've formed the group that will make up your co-op, all members should be required to sign a kind of constitution or pledge stating that they will abide by a set of basic guidelines. Here are some rules that most food co-ops find are essential:

• There should be absolutely no credit provided to co-op members. All goods must be paid for in cash or valid check, and if a family fails to pay, they should be dropped from the group automatically. A co-op is not a welfare society because it's been set up explicitly for mutual self-help, not charity. There are other channels people can use if they want to make a donation to the helpless or needy.

• All food purchased must be picked up at a central distribution point within a specified time period, usually twenty-four hours or less. If a member fails to pick up the food within that time period, he or she either forfeits the food or is dropped from the co-op. The reason for this is that the drop-off point is usually rotated among the homes and apartments of the other members, and nobody should be required to store somebody else's groceries.

• Everyone in the co-op should contribute a portion of his and her time equitably. Also, the various jobs should be shifted regularly from family to family, so that no one gets stuck with the most time-consuming task for an unfair period. A key requirement for membership in any food co-op is that each member must be willing to devote a fair share of time to the project. For those who try to get a free ride out of the efforts of others, or who would rather pay substitutes to fill in when the time comes around to work, a co-op won't be a good idea at all.

• Each person in the co-op must agree to be totally honest with all the other members. If there is a feeling of discontent about any matter in which the co-op is involved, that gripe should be put on the table as soon as possible so that it can be discussed fully and resolved. Because of the close working relationship that develops among co-op members, there are many opportunities for disagreements and hard feelings to arise. The purpose of a co-op is both economic and social. When one fails, so does the other.

The procedure used to divide up responsibilities and buy food should go something like this:

Step One: Locate and Price Foods. Appoint one person to approach wholesale and retail suppliers as a spokesperson for the group. Some suppliers will give group discounts and some won't, and it's important to determine which is which. Many times, a large independent retailer will sell cases of food to a co-op for a small markup. This advance person should also try to get price sheets on all products if they are available. If price sheets aren't available, they must be developed. This brings us to the next step: selecting the food items.

Step Two: Develop a Shopping List. One member of the co-op should be assigned the job of consolidating the price lists gathered by the advance person and then circulating these lists around to each member. The members should indicate which items they prefer in order of priority, as well as the maximum quantities they would like to purchase. The shopping-list coordinator must next go over all the lists and come up with a master shopping list based on the overall preferences of the group. According to estimates of those with experience in this sort of buying, it takes four hours of work to get to this point in the buying process. Items selected that add up to less than whole case lots should be dropped from the list because small purchases don't add up to decent savings.

Step Three: Buy and Pick up the Food. At least two other members of the group are responsible for collecting

the checks or money from each of the members and purchasing the food from the various suppliers selected. At
least one other member, with access to a van or pickup
truck, arranges to transport their purchases back to a central distribution point.

Step Four: Distribute the Food. Finally, a member's
garage or home is chosen as the pickup point for the food,
and as we've mentioned, all the goods should be picked up
within the determined period of time, or penalties, such as
loss of food, are assessed on those who fail to comply.

*Step Five: Keep a Simple Set of Books on Your
Purchases.* Complex bookkeeping is definitely not required
for food co-op purchases, and in fact, you will probably
find you can get along quite well without keeping any
books at all.

It's wise to keep some record of your purchases for at
least two reasons: In the first place, it will be helpful later
on to see just how much money has been saved and to
evaluate whether the saving really makes the co-op worth-
while. And secondly, many co-ops have discovered that
food costs run in cycles in their areas during the course of
a year. By reviewing their records, they can learn how to
buy certain items in quantity during the low cycles and
save even more money.

These guidelines aren't the result of some abstract
theory. On the contrary, they have developed as a result
of practical experiences of people involved in actual food
co-ops throughout the country.

For example, one food co-op I encountered, consisting
of people in the upper-middle income range, has desig-
nated two women members who are excellent bargain

shoppers to buy large quantities of products they find on sale. But these shoppers are authorized to buy without having to notify the other members first. Now, as you can imagine, the members of this group know each other very well—they understand each other's personal tastes and the amount of money that will be available for any given purchase.

On a number of occasions, these women have gone shopping for "closeout" meats on Mondays. These are meats that have turned a little brown and won't last much longer on the grocery shelves, but are still quite edible. The shoppers may buy out an entire counter, which amounts to three or four hundred pounds of meat, at rock-bottom prices. Then they immediately arrange to have the meat taken to a large food freezer which the group rents from a storage company. This kind of buying saves much more money than simply buying meats on regular supermarket sales. It's only possible because of mutual trust and sensitivity among these food co-op members.

This particular co-op also makes regular contact with refrigerator transportation companies in their area to see if any bargains have popped up. On one occasion, they learned that a truck had shipped some perishable foods to their city by mistake instead of to another city, and the entire truckload was up for sale. So they arranged to buy an entire truck of Cornish hens at only ten cents each!

Another technique that some canny co-op shoppers use is to look for culls, vegetables and fruits that have been tossed aside by canning and packing plants because they are cosmetically imperfect or too ripe for shipping. My wife and I have done this ourselves in certain sections of North Carolina, where my family vacations. For example, we once approached a tomato packing plant and asked about the culls that were available. The owner said, "I'll sell them to you for a dollar and thirty-five cents a box"— as compared with the regular price of three dollars a box. Needless to say, we bought as many as we could carry and sold the ones we couldn't use to friends.

This, then, is an overview of what's involved in setting up a food co-op. If you try it and find you like operating with other people this way, you may find you've opened the door to an extremely wide range of money-saving ventures. The second kind of cooperative program I want to discuss is a logical next step after you've succeeded with a food co-op.

The Equipment Cooperative. This kind of economic community sharing plan is a little more complex than the food co-op because it involves the use of shared tools and equipment. It is important that the individuals participating be completely compatible. So it's probably a good idea to try the food co-op first, and if you're satisfied it works smoothly, then move on to sharing certain types of equipment.

One natural outgrowth of the food co-op is the sharing of canning equipment to process fresh vegetables during the growing season. With proper planning, the equipment can be shared by all the members who are interested. Or the tasks can be divided, with some people planning the menus, some buying and picking up the products and others doing the canning.

One major advantage of a canning program is that you can bargain directly with farmers and farmers' market sellers in sizable enough quantities to get much lower prices by completely bypassing the markups associated with retailing. To acquire the practical skills, a person can enroll in one of the canning schools available through local colleges and adult education courses. One member can learn the method and then pass the skills on to others in the cooperative.

I've had some wary people object, "But how do you know that these people who are doing the canning are being careful in their work? Isn't there a chance of getting food poisoning from another person's canning job?"

There are a couple of ways to be certain of the safety of the canned foods you eat. First of all, when a jar is sealed properly, the lid recesses and maintains a concave structure. And when it is opened, you hear air pressure being released from inside. If the lid isn't concave and there is no release of pressure, then don't use that jar.

But perhaps an even more ironclad way to be sure is what I call the "General Patton Safety Principle." It seems that General George Patton was having problems with parachute packers in one of his commands: occasionally when his paratroopers jumped, the chutes didn't open.

So the general got into the habit of showing up unannounced in the parachute packing room and ordering the packers, "Pick up that last parachute you packed and come with me!" He would then take them to a waiting airplane, have them don the chutes, and when the plane reached several thousand feet, force them to jump.

From the time he instituted this procedure, he had no more problems with parachute packers—for obvious reasons. And the same principle can be applied to food canning: Those who do the canning are going to eat along with the others. I have never heard of a problem in a co-op where members shared equally.

But the opportunities for sharing equipment aren't limited to canning equipment. You may also find that you want to try some cooperative farming, perhaps on a tract of tillable land that one of the co-op members owns. Those who actually get into growing their own food often find it's an enjoyable and invigorating venture.

But let me offer a few words of warning: A great deal more time and equipment are required for this sort of venture than for the relatively simple food co-op, and each member should thoroughly evaluate such a commitment before any concrete plans are laid. Also, be sure to start out small, with a little plot that will require a minimum of time and effort from your members. Then you can feel your way along slowly and see which person fits best into which role, and what minimum equipment is necessary to operate a farming co-op.

As with all other cooperative ventures, this one should be conducted on a cash-only basis. If you get into a credit situation, where some members are paying and others are charging, hard feelings are sure to develop.

One of the advantages of this cooperative farming idea is that several families bear the financial burden of purchasing equipment that no single family could afford to own. And along the same lines, it's also possible for members to set up a "tool pool," where they chip in to buy gardening tools and other household equipment and then pass the equipment around for general use by those families participating in the venture.

If you try this neighborhood pooling concept, though, I would advise you to stay away from equipment that families use on a regular basis, such as lawnmowers and hand tools. The problem with these kinds of items is that they are needed frequently by nearly everyone, and they break down more frequently than seasonal or occasional-use equipment. As a result, someone inevitably ends up paying for something he hardly gets a chance to use. On the other hand, hardware such as tune-up equipment, seed spreaders, chain saws and similar items is much better suited to a cooperative sharing arrangement.

Another overlooked but still extremely helpful kind of product that a co-op might want to buy is a set of repair and maintenance books for use by the entire group. Sometimes, volumes of this type are available from your local library. But often, if you want a very specialized reference work, the book may not be available for one reason or another. So if you can develop a set of how-to books that can be spread out among your members, you'll find you can save a great deal of money that you might otherwise be tempted to put into high-priced hardbacks. Too many people I know buy practical volumes that they really need for a specific project, but they only use them for a few hours and then place them on a shelf to gather dust. A book pool is a great way to reduce these costs. A standard library check-out system should be employed to track the use of books and manuals, as well as the equipment itself.

The Community Clothes Closet and Swap Shop. Another important way to use a community sharing program is to set up a "community clothes closet" and also a "swap shop" for clothing. The difference between the two is that the clothes closet is a benevolent venture, where members contribute clothing to a central location so that those who are in need can pick it up *without any charge*. The swap shop, on the other hand, is a low-level barter arrangement where individuals who contribute items get credits which they can use to "purchase" other articles in the shop.

The advantage of setting up systems like these is that often one family will have items that are in good shape but are no longer needed. Unfortunately, they often don't know another family in their service organization with a need, so they may just let the goods sit or sell them at a flea market for practically nothing. By developing a community closet or swap shop, the gap between those who have the goods and those who need them can be bridged.

The best place to establish a clothes closet or thrift shop is in a church or organization room that can be set aside exclusively for this purpose. The size of the room will obviously vary depending on the size of the swap shop. Some operations like this can easily be housed in a literal closet, while others require several hundred square feet of space and a staff of full-time volunteers.

The benevolent clothes closet is a fairly easy concept to understand and requires little expertise. Those who have extra clothes or other usable items just drop them off at the special room or location set aside for the charitable distribution. If the clothes closet is operating under the umbrella of a recognized charity, the contributions can qualify as charitable donations which are deductible on income tax returns at an amount based on the fair market value of the items. To be certain that the donors get their full charitable deduction, it's important that they be given a receipt describing the articles donated. It is usually the responsibility of the donor to have the articles appraised to determine their value.

The barter-based swap shop is a little more complex than the clothes closet because the people who participate expect to exchange goods. The easiest way to conduct a swap shop is to require that those who bring items to exchange select something else on hand of approximately equivalent value. Then the exchange is made right on the spot.

The problem is that often people who bring in goods don't find anything they want right then. They may have to wait a few days or even weeks until a needed item comes in. So the most successful swap shops usually set up a system of credits which are assigned to each piece of property that arrives. Those participating in the swap system then have the right to "buy" anything with the credits they've accumulated. A simple transaction might look like this:

- Family A leaves shoes and receives ten credits.

- Family B leaves a man's suit and receives ten credits.

- Family A then uses their ten credits to obtain the suit.

- Family B isn't interested in the shoes that A left, but they decide a week or so later to trade their credits for several infant's outfits.

As you glance over this sample transaction, several procedural questions may come to mind. For example, how do you decide what different items are worth? And what happens if somebody contributes an item that nobody else wants?

There's no simple method to establish a uniform pricing system in a swap shop, especially if you begin to stock a variety of goods other than clothing, such as sports equipment or furniture. Most successful cooperatives limit the kinds of goods available until they get enough experience to take on other items—and this is one of the reasons I suggest that you stick to clothing at first.

Generally speaking, the items in the swap shop should be priced with the original retail price in mind when possible. This makes it easier to determine what the various goods are worth in relation to each other. For example, a suit that sells for $150 and is still in good shape might now be tagged at one third of retail, or $50. And if the shop elects to follow the simple system of making one shop credit equal to one dollar, the suit would now go for fifty credits.

It's best to have no more than two people doing the pricing because they will tend to balance each other when they have a difference of opinion. Yet their disagreements will most likely get resolved more quickly than if a committee tries to do the same job. Also, when several people are doing the pricing in separate small groups, the variations in price are usually extreme. The actual pricing is not critical, but uniformity in pricing is.

After the "prices" are selected, the pricers should evaluate and tag each item as soon as possible after it's presented. They should also remember that the *absolute* value placed on an item isn't important—only its *relative* value in comparison with other goods in the shop is an issue. The reason for this is that people who use the shop aren't going to be using money; they'll only use credits that reflect the relative value of items in the shop.

Individuals who contribute goods to the shop should be informed that the prices put on the items aren't negotiable. If they think the prices aren't high enough, return the items immediately. But if they agree with the pricing decision, then it's important to tag each item with the donor's swap shop ID number, the date submitted and the credit value. This information should also be entered into a donor record file. Tags can be made out with multiple carbon copies and will greatly simplify your record-keeping system.

As soon as an item is "sold," the tag on it should be removed and put in the donor's file along with a formal entry that he or she has received the appropriate number of swap shop credits. I would suggest that you *not* give a person credit for a contributed item until it's sold because it may never be sold. Most swap shops have a definite policy on unsold goods: If an item has been around for a prescribed period of time—usually no more than three months—it should be returned to the donor to make room for more usable goods.

The staffing for a swap shop will vary according to the number of goods to be handled. But as with every other crucial economic sharing community, I would suggest that you start small. A couple of volunteers to handle the exchange of goods and also to do the pricing should be enough to start out. Then, if the shop grows, other helpers can always be added, including perhaps someone to write and distribute a swap-shop bulletin to publicize goods on hand and goods needed to keep the transactions moving along.

As I have mentioned, this swap-shop concept is a simple variation on the barter transaction that was introduced earlier. The barters discussed there were quite complex and involved big corporations or even governments as participants. But there are also ways to expand this barter idea among individuals and small economic communities, and that's the topic I'd like us to turn our attention to now.

The Small Community Barter System. A complete barter system will include not only exchanges of clothing but also an exchange of other goods and of services as well. At this point, though, there are very few true non-commercial barter systems in operation that deal in services or a wide variety of retail products, and there are a couple of good reasons why.

First of all, running a barter system that includes exchanges of services or widely divergent products is hard to manage and requires rather complex records to keep track of all the transactions. And secondly, most people can still get along without a barter program. In other words, they don't feel an overwhelming need to shift from a money to a barter exchange system to make ends meet.

But there are several good reasons to consider getting involved in at least a simple community barter system. For one thing, a barter connection is a good insurance policy if a currency collapse occurs, because with such a system, you are using independent credits rather than the nation's questionable money supply.

Also, I've discovered in my counseling that many families are in much worse financial shape than they realize. And they can make good use of a barter arrangement to cut costs and build a surplus for investment.

How does a community barter system work?

The model you can begin with is the clothing swap shop we discussed a few pages back. But when you start to include services and very different kinds of goods, the pricing system gets more complex and will take more time and skill on the part of the volunteers.

The number of families involved in a barter exchange may be as small as two: For example, a teenager who wants piano lessons may trade baby-sitting services for a piano teacher's time. But obviously the larger the group, the greater the variety of barter trades that will be possible. By my estimates, a group of about 150 families selected at random will represent a self-sufficient economic system, with the majority of necessary services and goods available somewhere in the community.

As the barter concept expands from a simple clothes-swapping arrangement to a variety of goods and services, it becomes increasingly important to keep good records. All trades have to be precisely accounted for if every participant is to get a fair value from the association, and the most successful communities usually find that it eventually becomes necessary to hire a part-time bookkeeper—preferably one whose services have been bartered for within the system. It may also be helpful to purchase one of the small, relatively inexpensive personal computers to keep track of the transactions. Like other goods and services, your group may be able to get the use of a computer owned by one of your members in exchange for barter credits.

As for assigning values to various goods and services, try to follow the basic swap-shop method described earlier. Decide on the average retail value for services and goods and discount these values if the goods are secondhand or the services are adequate but not quite at the top professional level.

Obviously, the pricing of services may vary widely, involve many subjective judgments and also get extremely expensive—especially if you have lawyers or doctors who want to contribute their professional skills. If service values are inflated just so that an individual can take advantage of the barter exchange, then the system will fail. So it's important to have an independent appraisal of values and also to have an understanding among the members that the prices should be kept as low as possible to

101

make the barter exchange more attractive than regular cash transactions on the outside.

Although a bulletin or other publication may only be optional for the simple clothing swap shop, it becomes essential for the more extensive community barter system. A regular newsletter should advertise the services and goods available and their trade costs. But like other aspects of running an economic community service, a newsletter takes money and manpower. Even a mimeographed, single-sheet monthly report will require several days to compile, type, print and mail. Initially, your group should be prepared to spend about $50 to $100 per month for materials and mailing costs and for the services—or bartered service credits—of two people for eight hours an issue.

I've already described in some detail the possible tax implications of barter transactions, and I'll leave it up to you to decide how you feel about the IRS rulings on barter clubs. The rulings are not law, by the way, but the IRS may require you to go to court if you disagree with their position that all barter exchanges are taxable. Even if community barter systems result in totally taxable exchanges, there are still significant benefits for you and your neighbors. For example, if you're in a high tax bracket of say 50 percent, your maximum tax would only be 50 percent of the "average value" of the goods or services you receive—a figure that would be much less than their full retail value, which you would have to pay on the open market. Also, the goods you swap may be deducted as your "cost of goods sold."

For further information on setting up a community barter system, you may want to write to Barter Project, c/o Volunteer, National Center for Citizen Involvement,

1214 16th Street, Washington, D.C. 20036. Among other things, this group will send you a bimonthly newsletter called *Exchange Networks*.

Barter systems are clearly more effective if individual members have special skills, especially in repair and maintenance fields, which they can exchange with other members. Also, as long as these skills are different from what the person does in his regular business, the exchanges are more likely to be tax-free transactions, and thus more valuable to those involved in the barter project.

But before you can trade a service or skill, it's obviously necessary to have one or acquire one. So let's turn to some of the ways you can learn to "work underground"—both to enhance your bartering position and also to build up capital to invest or to give away.

CHAPTER EIGHT

The Underground Job Market

The economic power of America was built in large part on the shoulders of the small entrepreneur—the strong individualist who, with a minimum of capital but an over-supply of self-confidence and hard work, pushed and promoted his way to business success.

The ideal of the Horatio Alger hero, who goes from rags to riches by dint of nothing more than his wit and grit, has become a fixed part of American folklore. Unfortunately, this compelling, independent entrepreneur is now more the exception than the rule in our business world.

A few individualistic men and women are striking out on their own every day to try to establish new businesses that will provide them with more control over their lives, as well as an opportunity to make it big in purely financial terms. But most Americans cling to the seeming security of jobs with established companies and fear cutting those corporate ties that provide them with comfortable fringe benefits and regular weekly paychecks.

Alexis de Tocqueville, that Frenchman of the 1830's who traveled across America and then committed his observations to paper in *Democracy in America*, would probably not have recognized any connection between our nation today and the country of his time. Commenting on American business ventures, for example, he said, ". . . what most astonishes me in the United States is not so much the marvelous grandeur of some undertakings as the innumerable multitude of small ones."

There are still many "small undertakings" in our time. But De Tocqueville would have been more impressed by our massive corporations and huge government agencies that reach into so many parts of our lives. Yet the fact that we have drifted from smallness to bigness in many of our ventures doesn't mean that it's *better* to be big than small. On the contrary, we've lost a great deal as the average person's inclination to strike out on his own has declined.

It's important to try to recapture some of the spirit that helped make us a great nation economically. There are still a handful of hard-driving, creative, independent-minded workers who move out on their own and make it big—or at least achieve some degree of success—with their own businesses. But for the most part, these people are the exception rather than the rule, and their approach to work isn't generally known or understood by the average American. The popular press runs periodic articles on entrepreneurial exploits, but most people don't have any direct experience with independent free enterprise. That's why, when you take a chance on jumping feet first into an independent, self-employed venture, you're working underground. This means trying to find your way around in a subterranean region that has few maps or guides but that holds the promise of great treasure—if you are just persistent and exercise good judgment on the journey.

Every reader of this book—and that includes you—should be involved in some kind of self-employed venture. That doesn't mean you have to dream up a business idea tonight and quit your job tomorrow to pursue it. But it does mean that you should start moving into some sort of independent enterprise immediately, even if it remains only a sideline or a hobby.

But why make the effort? Why not just find some big, comfortable corporation with a pension plan, insurance program and other benefits, and forget all the hassles often associated with starting up your own business? There are very good reasons for not following this course. Here are some of the factors that motivate me to urge you toward self-employment:

There's a trend toward later retirement in this country. This movement has been noted in a number of reports that have been publicized recently. For example, a survey by the Travelers Insurance Companies of Hartford showed that 43 percent of their employees aged sixty-two to sixty-five plan to keep working past the age of sixty-five.

There are a number of reasons suggested for this trend. For one thing, inflation has cut into fixed pension benefits, and so most people require some ongoing source of income to maintain a semblance of their preretirement life-style. Having your income tied to some sort of compensation for services that increases with the general rise of wages and prices gives you a built-in hedge against inflation.

Also, as people live longer and enjoy relatively good

health into their later years, they find they want to keep a hand in the working world in some way—at least as a part-time, if not full-time, worker. Finally, even the most conservative estimates project that the percentage of the population sixty-five years old and older will have doubled between 1960 and 2010, and this probably means reductions in Social Security and other retirement benefits, since two out of three Americans will be eligible for retirement.

What all this means is that it will be extremely helpful if you learn to work underground in your own self-employed venture before you reach retirement age so that you don't have to rely on some big corporation or other employer to feed you.

Having a special independent skill puts you in a stronger position to trade your services in a barter economy. Suppose you decide to learn auto repair, woodworking or secretarial skills. Any of these abilities will give you a strong foundation for exchanging something you can do to help others for something they can do to assist you. As a result, your skill will enable you to cut your costs for outside services and free more money to invest or give away.

An independent secondary job provides great job security. There are at least two ways that you can increase your personal security by working underground. In the first place, you may lose your present job at some point in the future. If that happens, an alternate occupation, which may have been just a moonlighting venture or even a hobby, can become your regular employment and help tide you over until you get back into the regular job market again.

108

But there's also security in the knowledge that if a currency collapse occurs later and you lose your job at that time, you'll have a solid fallback position with your entrepreneurial "underground" pursuit. One of the main advantages of being self-employed during a collapse is that nobody can fire you if times get tough. Your business may fall off. But unless the work you have chosen is extremely vulnerable to a troublesome economy, you'll probably still be able to put food on the table.

These, then, are some basic reasons for working underground. Now, in concrete terms, how do you go about doing it?

In my own working life and also in counseling thousands of working people during the past years I've discovered some principles that I call the *Eight Basic Guidelines for Working Underground.* I could never guarantee you'll become a millionaire if you follow these guidelines, but I do believe you'll have the best chance of getting your own business off the ground if you make them a part of your game plan.

1. *Transform yourself into an entrepreneur.* "Lazy hands make a man poor, but diligent hands bring wealth." (Prov. 10:4)

Some people have more natural talent than others in business. But anybody can become a successful small-business person by just setting his or her mind to it. Entrepreneurs, in other words, are made, not born. You just have to acquire the know-how to turn yourself into one.

There are some seminars and other courses, sponsored both by business schools and by independent groups like the Entrepreneur Institute, that give instruction in how to start and run your own business. And it might be worth your while to attend one of these workshops to get some formal education in this area before you embark on your own venture.

But many people can achieve the same result by keeping in mind advice like that given by Professor Karl H. Vesper, of the University of Washington at Seattle. When asked by *Forbes* magazine what he thinks it takes to be a successful entrepreneur, Professor Vesper said there are six "critical things": (1) a concept of the enterprise in terms of the product or service you'll offer, (2) technical know-how, (3) physical resources, such as adequate capital, to get your venture off the ground, (4) supportive people to help you make the right decisions and keep on a profitable track, (5) customer orders in hand before you begin, and (6) time to put all these things into effect.

Professor Vesper puts a heavy emphasis on the time element because often entrepreneurs start their businesses off on a part-time basis and then devote all their after-work energies to it. The problem with this approach is that all the other demands of your life may get in the way and you'll fail to put in the minimum time to give your entrepreneurial idea a fair chance.

You may have noticed, by the way, that Vesper didn't include risk as one of his key elements, even though many people often think of risk-taking as the prime characteristic of the independent business person. It's true that it always requires some risk to try a new venture all by yourself, but the interesting thing, Vesper notes, is that many of the entrepreneurs he knows haven't been aware of the risk. In other words, they didn't think, "Now the time has come for me to take a big risk." They just move ahead, so the willingness to take a risk wasn't a factor in their decision to start a business.

2. *When you pick an underground business, think in terms of those that will be collapse-proof.* "The prudent see danger and take refuge, but the simple keep going and suffer for it." (Prov. 27:12)

You may like acting or writing or opera singing. But unless you have a foothold in those fields to begin with, it's best not to regard them as your chosen field of work in the underground economy because you may never have even the slightest chance of making a living in those jobs.

It's much better to try to anticipate what types of work will be most likely to survive and thrive during and after a monetary collapse, and then to launch your entrepreneurial venture in those areas. For example, if times get tough and people have little money because they're out of work or the money they have isn't worth much because of runaway inflation, they probably won't be buying many new goods. Instead, they'll be trying to make do on the old appliances and equipment they have. So if you develop an expertise in any sort of repair or maintenance field, you'll have a ready-made outlet for your services.

For example, one man I know owned a large auto dealership that sold mainly Chryslers. He sensed that Chrysler was in economic trouble and might even go out of business, so he decided he'd better look for some sort of "insurance" in case he found himself without any more cars to sell. We discussed his problem extensively and he finally concluded, "Cars are all I know, and my repair service and used-car department at the dealership are doing well. So why not begin to stress those sides of the business more?"

As a result of this decision, he started buying wrecked cars which had less than 20,000 miles on them and also were less than two years old. He got the autos at very low prices and then rebuilt them and sold them at an excellent profit. Now he has a staff of people going around the country finding these wrecks for him, and he's even developed a do-it-yourself kit for his customers in case they want to save themselves even more money by putting in their own labor. He's now in the enviable position that the worse the economy gets, the better his business becomes.

But repair and maintenance work are only some of the more obvious collapse-proof fields. Strange as it seems to many people, another extremely good area during a downturn is recreation. I tracked four of the major downturns in the last couple of decades rather closely, and I found that the recreational industries were among the most profitable. Attendance at movies and restaurants was up, as was participation in sports like racket ball. And sporting-goods businesses often experience mini-booms.

I'm not sure of the reason for this phenomenon. Perhaps people are looking for an escape from the pressures and disappointments of their working lives. Or maybe there isn't enough money to take long trips to major resorts, so people cut back and spend what extra funds they have on local recreation.

My stepfather is a good example of how you can take advantage of the part-time job opportunities in recreation, especially if you have a sports orientation. He's a retired Navy chief, but even with his retirement income he always looks for ways to get a little extra cash. The problem is that he didn't want to tie himself down to one particular part of the country because, after all, he *is* retired and wants to enjoy the freedom that can come with some amount of pension income.

So he finally settled on baseball umpiring. Even though he had never played baseball, he had attended many games and loved the sport. Also, the field fits his personality because he likes to assume control in activities in which he participates, and he has little fear of rejection—an important quality for an umpire! So he went to umpire school and now umpires baseball and softball games in Florida during the early months of the year and then moves up to North Carolina with my mother to pick up the later season there. This job gives him great independence over his schedule because he can pick and choose where he works. And also he knows he can get work for six or seven months out of the year to supplement his regular retirement income.

The possibilities for collapse-proof entrepreneurial enterprises are almost endless. It's just a matter of sitting down and going over your own abilities and interests and then matching them with fields that you think may be likely to make it through an economic problem period.

3. No job is too menial in the underground economy. "A man's pride brings him low, but a man of lowly spirit gains honor." (Prov. 29:23)

Many people have missed great opportunities to have an exciting occupational adventure and also to build highly successful businesses because they weren't willing to get their hands dirty. Our notions about work have become highly stratified in recent years, especially among the white-collar middle class, so that many of us aren't

113

willing to take on lowly chores which may be necessary to get a new business on its feet.

We Americans weren't always like this, however. I like the way Alexis de Tocqueville put it in his descriptions of the early nineteenth-century worker:

"In America no one is degraded because he works, for everyone about him works also; nor is anyone humiliated by the notion of receiving pay, for the President of the United States also works for pay. He is paid for commanding, other men for obeying orders. In the United States professions are more or less laborious, more or less profitable; but they are never either high or low: every honest calling is honorable."

Most of the successful and financially secure entrepreneurs I know have this attitude. They also believe that all work is honorable, and they're willing to pitch in and do almost anything if their labors will help them further along toward the goal of transforming their business enterprise into a highly profitable operation.

One friend of mine always spoke with some pride and respect about his father's approach to work. His dad was a financial vice president for a number of companies in the Southwest before his death, but he never became so impressed by his own importance as an executive that he felt he absolutely *had* to have a high-level job. This father was a pragmatist who once told his son, "I'd never go without work just because I felt a job wasn't quite up to the image I have of myself. I once pumped gas for a living when I was a young fellow, and I'd do the same thing again if that was the only way I could earn a living for my family."

And even though he never went back to the gas pump, he did have to take a job just before his death that some might think had less status than some of his earlier positions. But, true to his word, he threw himself into his tasks as cheerfully and diligently as if he were once again at the top of the corporate heap.

This principle of looking at all work as honorable reminds me of a story involving a leading cardiologist in a big city. He heard from one of his kids that the upstairs toilet was overflowing, so he rushed to the phone book in a panic and called up a local plumber. The plumber immediately came over and went up to the bathroom, but all he did was pull out one little tool, reach down into the toilet and solve the problem after about three minutes of work.

"Okay, doc, that will be seventy-five dollars," the plumber said as he stood up to leave.

"For goodness sake, I'm a doctor and I don't earn seventy-five dollars for three minutes work!" the cardiologist protested.

The plumber smiled at him and said, "You know, doc, I didn't earn that much when I was a doctor either!"

The thing I like about this story is that it suggests that all honest work is worth a reasonable wage. And in fact, seemingly lowly, blue-collar labor—such as fixing toilets —may, at the right time and right place, lead to riches and financial security even more quickly than professions that require much more education and confer higher social status.

This is the way I'd like you to start thinking as you consider possible alternate job outlets for yourself in the underground economy. Forget the image you think you have in your social circle right now. Free yourself from living by the drumbeat that others are marching to, and let your mind roam free, perhaps in those areas that you now enjoy as a hobby—or think you might enjoy. And you might even play a sort of game with yourself: As you read your favorite newspapers and magazines each week, or engage in conversations or other encounters with your friends, keep your eyes open for possible entrepreneurial schemes that you could transform into a going enterprise in your spare time.

One fellow I know who took this approach was a professional athlete who realized he was reaching the end of his short sports career. So he started to look around for another occupation, and an idea finally came to him from an unexpected quarter—a fire which burned part of a friend's apartment.

He noticed that after the work of the firemen and the fire, his friend had had much of his furniture severely damaged. The insurance company told his friend to have the furniture refurbished and they would pay for it, so the friend went out to see what he could find in the way of refurbishing services in his city. He learned there were only about three companies in the city that engaged in this business, and they were all booked up. It was going to cost thousands of dollars to get the furniture redone, and there would be a minimum wait of nine months before the job could be finished.

As he followed this saga, the athlete started getting some ideas about what career he might pursue when he left pro sports. What he saw here was a business with an overload of work, high profits and not much competition. So he went to work learning how to refurbish furniture in his off season.

In the view of some of his colleagues, who were used to living high and spending much of their money on clothes and entertainment, this athlete's choice of an off-season career seemed quite a comedown. After all, how could

THE UNDERGROUND JOB MARKET

someone who had come to thrive on the cheers of thousands of fans be satisfied with sitting alone in the back room of some warehouse, sanding furniture?

But this athlete followed his vision of a second career, and his persistence paid off. The last I heard, he was out of professional athletics, but he was pulling down $100,000 a year refurbishing furniture. Not only that, he owns his own company—so his total assets come to much more than he ever owned when he was in sports.

My friend made his reputation by being able to fix furniture faster than anyone else in the city, and his firm is still growing by leaps and bounds. He was a person who accepted De Tocqueville's notion that all work is honorable—and he stuck by that conviction and let it carry him to great success, despite the sneers of some of his teammates.

So don't let your friends, family traditions or some phony image of yourself prevent you from taking a chance on an enterprise that could be financially fruitful, as well as just plain fun. After all, we're talking about *alternative* jobs, not your main profession, so you're free to try almost anything you'd like. And it's often those people with something of a renegade streak—and the courage to act on it —who turn an enjoyable sideline into a super-successful business.

4. There's often less risk in doing what you want to do, than in doing what you feel you ought to do. "For day and night your hand was heavy upon me; my strength was sapped as in the heat of summer." (Psalm 32:4)

Now, I realize this particular guideline is something of a mouthful, but think about it for a moment. You'll recall we discussed earlier how Professor Vesper of the University of Washington believes that, contrary to popular notions, a risk-taking mentality often isn't a central part of the personality of many successful entrepreneurs. And I would take that one step further: Sometimes it's a lot riskier to stay with a job which may, to outward appearances, seem successful, but which may be leaving you unfulfilled and even bored.

Let me explain with an example from my counseling experience. The president of a major bank in one large city came to me and said, "I sure am dissatisfied with what I do. I hate to sit in that office, wear my tie and three-piece suit and put up with all the phoniness and ladder climbing."

"What would you *like* to do?" I asked.

"Be a carpenter," he said. "But I can't afford to be a carpenter."

"You know what?" I said. "You can't afford *not* to be a carpenter! You can't afford not to do the thing that gives you the most peace and satisfaction. Tell me: What is it that makes you think you'll always be in the banking industry? If your bank has a major economic problem, whom will they replace?"

"Why, *me*," he said. He realized, as he thought about it, that he would be like the coach on a losing football team if his bank started to go downhill. He was the one who would get fired first.

He decided to mull over the issue for a while, and when I saw him about six months later, he said he had resigned as the chief executive officer of the bank and had gone to work as a carpenter's helper. The builder, it seems, was a friend of his and had wanted him to come on as a full partner. But the banker had wanted to learn the trade first, in a menial position. So he continued to work for two

118

years as a carpenter until he knew the business thoroughly, and then he accepted his friend's offer of a partnership.

At this point, the two of them have one of the soundest building programs I know of in the entire country. The former banker arranges all the buyers' loans and financing, and the builder handles the construction end of the business. They are one of the few building firms I know which build everything debt free, and even during economic downturns, they have continued to do a good business because they don't have to worry about paying off bank loans.

And there's an interesting conclusion to this story. The chief executive who took over for the banker was fired within eighteen months after he assumed office as president of the bank. The problem was that the country went into an economic tailspin in 1975 and the bank lost more money than it ever had in its history. And since the president was the "coach of the team," he was held responsible.

The same thing might well have happened to my friend if he had stayed with the bank. But because he chose to do what he wanted to do, rather than hanging on to a job that seemed to have higher status and more security, he ended up with more status and security than he had ever known—not to mention plenty of job satisfaction as well.

5. *Examine your hobbies for profit potential.* "Do you see a man skilled in his work? He will serve before kings; he will not serve before obscure men." (Prov. 23:29)

Often, the things that a person chooses to do in his spare time, not for pay but for the sheer enjoyment of the activity, may reflect an interest and expertise that can be turned into a business. One of the reasons for this is that if you're willing to spend time working hard at something when you have no expectation of pay, you're demonstrating a persistence and creative drive that are key elements in a successful entrepreneurial venture. One good example of how this works came to my attention a few years ago when a man who was dissatisfied with his work as a salesman came into my office for advice.

He had been having trouble holding down a job and was afraid he was on the verge of getting fired again—but he couldn't figure out what was wrong with him. As we talked, it became obvious that he wasn't cut out to be a salesman because he had a strong fear of rejection and wasn't aggressive about going out to make contacts. He preferred to spend his time at home in a woodworking shop he had set up in his basement.

Things got very bad at work and he was bringing in so few commissions that he had been forced to supplement his income by gathering old cast-off wood from barns and converting it into picture frames. In fact, he had even considered going into the picture-frame making business full-time until he started running out of barnwood.

As he and I talked, other ideas for woodworking-related businesses kept popping up, until we finally began to concentrate on an idea he had come across involving the construction of wooden solar collectors for an out-of-town manufacturer. He had apparently been visiting the home of a friend who had ordered one of the collectors, but the friend couldn't get delivery because the company was small and was having trouble meeting production schedules.

After seeing how simple the construction was, he wrote the owner of the company and said, "I have a small woodworking shop and I believe I can manufacture some of your solar boxes. Why don't you let me build one for a friend who has sent an order to you, and you can then evaluate whether or not my services might be useful?"

So the manufacturer agreed to try him out. They bought the materials for him for $50 and paid him another $50 to build the box, and he did such a good job that they immediately started sending him other orders to fill. The venture proved immediately profitable because he was able to build each box in about three hours, so he was making about $17 an hour, with much of his costs and overhead paid for.

This business relationship proved so productive that the salesman—who is no longer a salesman—moved to California to run a new plant for the manufacturer as a junior partner.

So in this man's case, something which had started out as a hobby turned into a lucrative part-time project and finally into his major business. Of course, it's not necessary that you think in terms of always turning your underground work into a major, full-time business. In fact, it's perfectly all right to keep it at the hobby level if you have other work or family responsibilities that are now taking up most of your time. The main idea is just to develop a sideline skill that you are able to turn into a money-making venture, if the need arises, at some point in the future. It's the insurance value of the underground work I'm mainly concerned about—not the immediate profit potential.

My wife is a good case in point. She's not particularly interested in embarking on a full-time work project right now, but she is interested in developing a skill that will give her some direction if something happened to me. So she has developed an expertise in making stained-glass plates and knickknacks and now keeps a complete set of manufacturing equipment in our garage.

She's developed enough of a skill and interest in this area that we are now looking around for possible sales outlets for her work, such as the network of Christian bookstores around the country. But in the meantime, she is probably the staunchest upholder of our family tradition of making, rather than buying, all the gifts we send off on Christmas and other special occasions. The quality of her handiwork is much more valuable and personal than anything we could afford to buy, and she's saving us a great deal of money by making the gift items herself.

6. *Learn to look for business ideas in the ordinary areas of your life.* "By wisdom a house is built, and through understanding it is established." (Prov. 24:3)

We've already touched upon this approach, as with the example of the pro athlete who first observed his friend's problems with having furniture refurbished and then acted on what he saw. But a few more words need to be said on this topic

If you train yourself to become more sensitive to what's going on around you, you'll be surprised how many entrepreneurial ideas will come to mind. It's a matter of training yourself to become more creative. There are two steps in the process. First, you need to learn to perceive the *needs* around you that aren't being met. And next, you have to teach yourself to speculate on ways you can fulfill those needs—and make some money in the process.

For example, I have one friend whose independent religious ministry was running into financial problems, so he decided he needed to try to earn some money on the side to sustain himself. He began to look around for things he could do in his spare time—things that wouldn't require too large an investment because he didn't have a lot of extra cash on hand.

One of the first things that struck him was also one of the most commonplace things in his life—his digital watch. The internal mechanism of the watch began to malfunction, and he tried to find a place that would repair it—but none was available in his city. He finally found that the only repair facility was in Buffalo, New York, and that he'd have to send his watch up there if he wanted to get it working again.

Then he began to wonder just how much trouble it was to learn to repair a digital watch, and he ended up writing the Buffalo office to find out if there was any way he could get into the digital watch repair business. The company sent him a telegram immediately and said, "We've been looking for someone to get into this business. How would you like to attend a school we run up here?"

The upshot of this interchange is that now he is making a good living on the side as a digital-watch repairman. The key principle, then, is to look for a vacuum that needs to be filled in the marketplace, and if you think your interests and skills can be marshaled to meet the need, get moving and make an opening for yourself!

7. *The enterprise you pick must fit your own special personality and background.* "An anxious heart weighs a man down, but a kind word cheers him up." (Prov. 12:25)

Perhaps this guideline seems too self-evident even to mention, but you'd be surprised at the number of people who consider getting involved in a business that requires doing something that, down deep, they really dislike.

One of the things that obscures a meaningful, objective

self-examination before beginning a new business is the overriding desire to make a lot of money. Now, there's nothing wrong with making money. In fact, there's a great deal that's right about it if your motives are right and are a by-product of doing something else that's meaningful. But if you are motivated primarily by a desire to become rich and ignore greater values, you may find yourself with a great business concept that's exactly wrong for you. And regardless of how the business does, you lose.

For example, you hear many rosy promises from those who promote person-to-person selling programs as a sure-fire plan for riches, and for some people these plans do fit their personalities perfectly. But if you're a thin-skinned person who is devastated whenever somebody turns you down for something, stay away from this kind of sales work! The only way you can become truly successful in person-to-person selling is to be persistent and play the percentages by expecting a majority of rejections in relation to successes. And it takes a special kind of personality to keep an upbeat, positive attitude in the face of such pressure.

So make the advice in Proverbs 10:22 your personal slogan as you're looking into possible entrepreneurial projects: "The blessing of the Lord brings wealth, and he adds no trouble to it." In other words, your work, whether your regular job or your underground occupation, should involve something you really enjoy and are cut out for. It's a miserable thing to wake up in the morning and dread going to the office. No amount of money can compensate you adequately for that.

8. Become a doer, not a dreamer. "The lazy man does

not roast his game, but the diligent man prizes his posses-sions." (Prov. 12:27)

This final guideline is here primarily to remind you that just reading this book isn't going to turn you into a great American entrepreneur. I've known so many people who were experts at brainstorming and speculating about dif-ferent business ideas, but who were never willing to take that first step to get their venture off the ground.

Part of the problem may be a lack of time, as Professor Vesper indicated in our first guideline describing some of the basics of becoming an effective entrepreneur. So for active and competent people, the most important initial step in any underground business program is probably just to clear your schedule so that you can sit down and plan your entrepreneurial venture.

But there's a great gulf between scribbling some notes in your armchair in front of the television set, and commit-ting a reasonable amount of time and money to the actual work it takes to begin a new business. You can always start small—such as beginning your business in a corner of your own home. And I would highly recommend that you increase your financial and overhead commitments very gradually.

But eventually, if you want to succeed, you'll have to devote a substantial chunk of time and effort to your idea. That's the only way your concept will get a really good test in the marketplace. One real estate salesman I know was running into some problems with his regular work because the economy was bad and had discouraged home buyers from committing themselves.

So he decided he needed to stabilize his income by get-ting into a supplementary field that would bring in some extra money when his regular real estate ventures were especially slow. Because in his part of the country the worst time for land sales was the late fall and winter, he started looking around for something he could pursue profitably from late November through March.

The idea he finally settled on was something he knew about and liked—gathering and selling firewood. He understood real estate and was aware of places that he could go to set up contracts for cutting firewood. And he also enjoyed being out of doors for a portion of the year.

But he didn't procrastinate. He could have spent weeks dreaming about how great it would be to shift to the great out-of-doors and become a modern-day Paul Bunyan. But instead of dreaming about it, he *did* it!

With a small truck, a log splitter and one employee, he began to cut trees down during his spare time in the late summer and early fall. Then during those winter months when his regular real estate business was off, he devoted all his time to selling the firewood in stands on the side of the highway.

Now, he earns about $40,000 a year in firewood sales during the winter, and that's his compensation after all his expenses and labor costs are paid. In some of the years since he's embarked on this venture, this "part-time" income has exceeded what he made from his regular job.

All of the individuals mentioned in this chapter have succeeded in working underground—and often have turned their alternative jobs into their main occupations —because they share certain common entrepreneurial strengths. Some have stumbled onto these qualities and principles accidentally or for some reason have grown up just naturally thinking like entrepreneurs. But others have sat down in counseling sessions or in periods of intense self-analysis and have taken time to learn the skills necessary for success in self-employment enterprises.

All family planning—including the formulation of a successful self-employment venture—requires the honest input of both husband and wife. Obviously, either spouse could come up with and be the primary implementer of a money-making idea. But too often, when it's the husband's brainchild, the wife is excluded from the planning phase of these entrepreneurial projects. Yet not only do women provide excellent insight and good balance, but also husband-wife communication remains the key to *all* effective family financial planning.

Everyone of average intelligence has the seeds of self-employment success. It's just a matter of cultivating those innate qualities and applying them in practice to the right kind of business project. One of the best ways to gain expertise in the entrepreneurial approach—which is an absolute prerequisite for working underground successfully—is to start early and try out new projects regularly until you finally hit pay dirt.

It's a good idea, for example, to introduce your children to the idea of learning some manual skill that will enable them to earn some money during their summer vacations or after school. My first son wants to go to law school, but in the meantime he's devoted much of his spare time to learning how to be an artist and draftsman. This training has given him an alternate skill which is very much in demand and which provides him with a reasonably secure fallback position in case something goes wrong with his primary career goals.

My second son wants to be an engineer, but he's not waiting around to get his degree before he learns a marketable trade. While in the Marine Corps Reserve, he went through a school for electronic technicians, so that he's able to repair radios, televisions, clocks and other appliances. And I can't think of a better collapse-proof field than this repair area.

My other two kids haven't yet settled on a secondary underground work field, but I expect them to before long. And even if they never use what they've learned to earn money, they will be in a strong position to help needy people who can't afford repairs or whatever. Also, they'll be able to barter their services if they should ever be inclined in that direction.

But perhaps the best thing about starting kids working underground at a young age is that it gives them practical training in thinking like an entrepreneur—training which has been largely lost in our contemporary age, but which is essential if you want them to be as secure as possible in our uncertain economy.

So now you know some of the ins and outs of the alternative work movement, and perhaps you already have a few part-time money-making ideas you'd like to pursue. Also, you know a great deal about such cash-conserving arrangements as barters and swap shops.

But what's the best way to manage all these surplus funds you've now started to generate—so that you can have a maximum amount for investment? For the answer to that question, let's turn first to a consideration of the most effective method for setting up a personal budget.

CHAPTER NINE

The
Bare-Bones Budget

The most successful of our early American predecessors knew exactly how much money came into their hands and how it could be spent wisely. They were budget conscious because, in many cases, they had risen from poverty and had no intention of slipping back in that direction a second time.

A quote from Proverbs 24:33–34 best expresses the need for keeping both your eyes open where money is concerned:

> *A little sleep, a little slumber,*
> *a little folding of the hands to rest—*
> *and poverty will come on you like a bandit*
> *and scarcity like an armed man.* (NIV)

Nobody assumed that there should be an all-powerful government to provide for those who were foolish enough to neglect their own families. Each individual was ultimately responsible for taking care of himself. This attitude was balanced by an assurance that God was the ultimate source of all provision and would supply what was needed.

Benjamin Franklin captured this principle rather nicely when he wrote in *Poor Richard's Almanack* about the importance of applying thrift and wisdom as you tend to even the smallest details of personal finances:

> *Nor trivial loss, nor trivial gain despise;*
> *Molehills, if often heaped, to Mountains rise:*
> *Weigh every small Expence, and nothing waste,*
> *Farthings long sav'd, amount to Pounds at last.*

Such adages, though they may seem old-fashioned to many people today, were accepted as basic truths of life a hundred years ago or more in our country. Yet in recent times, with our increasingly "sophisticated" ways of doing business—including our plastic-money credit cards, our bank draft overdraw accounts and the endless variety of ways we can get loans or "leverage" our existing assets—we tend to discount such precepts. I can remember one young lawyer who, after reading a book on the business world, criticized a section of the text for taking "too strong a position in favor of the old work ethic idea."

That's astounding, isn't it? It's amazing, and even alarming, that present-day Americans often seem reluctant to accept and apply long-standing, self-evident truths about their personal finances. And they reject these tried and true principles on the flimsy ground that they must be defective simply because they arose and gained respect at some point in the past. Instead of recognizing that our contemporary civilization stands on the shoulders of what has come before, many people seem to think we should just ignore all our intellectual and practical roots.

But that's wrong.

We should study and build on what was good and successful in our past. And having a sound family budget was definitely one of the basic truths which our most successful parents and grandparents observed. So what I want to do in this chapter is help you glean some of the key underlying principles from those traditional, tested budget practices and then learn to apply them in your own life. Finally, when you lay a solid budgetary foundation for your family, you'll find you have a firm platform from which you can take full advantage of other areas of the underground economy.

First of all, let me lay down the basic precepts that will be guiding us through this discussion of your personal budget. Some of these ideas may seem strange—or even downright radical—because they're so different from the common approach to financial planning. In fact, one of the reasons that I include this section on budgeting as an integral part of the underground economy is that it's definitely *not* a part of our current economic training.

You'll find that you have to ignore much of the previous advice you've heard and erroneous assumptions you've made about such things as credit in order to realize true financial freedom and security. These aren't new theories. They are tried and proven principles that were common practice prior to fifty years ago.

Principle One: Get Out of Debt and Stay Out. If you'll think about this principle for a moment or two before reading any further, you'll realize how radical a concept it is. It runs contrary to the advice of most tax planners and consultants. It means doing something that runs counter to much of the "common wisdom" that we hear in conversations, television ads and our daily banking and business transactions. As a matter of fact, if you *really* think about this idea, you may find yourself asking, "How can a person even *exist* in our society without being in debt?"

At first, it's sometimes hard to go against the grain of the "accepted" social and financial practices. But it's these so-called accepted practices that have brought us to the brink of financial disaster. We'll look at a few ways that you can organize your personal finances, your income and outflow of funds, so that you'll not only be able merely to exist without any debt, but actually to prosper as a result. In other words, you don't need to deprive yourself and your family of all the good things of life and embark on some sort of ascetic program of total self-denial.

On the contrary, you should do what Benjamin Franklin suggested in that little aphorism quoted at the beginning of this chapter, that is, put together an easy-to-maintain personal budget that will enable you to monitor every "trivial loss" and take full advantage of every "trivial gain," as he put it. In this way, you'll be able to get the maximum use of each dollar that comes into your hands, and you'll begin to develop a surplus of funds that will give you the freedom to do things you could never afford on your old system of managing money.

But now, back to the problem of debt. Indebtedness is *owing more money than you can reasonably pay back*. For example, a simple mortgage on your home does not constitute a "debt." It just means that you have a contract to make payments on an appreciating asset—your residence. It's only when you can't comfortably meet those contractual obligations that you run into debt problems. (I adhere to a rather unique philosophy about home owner-ship which we'll get into shortly. But for our present pur-poses it is sufficient to say that if your mortgage payments fit within your budget, home ownership is a practical alter-native to renting.)

Another factor that reflects a problem debt situation is *an obligation to make payments on items that are not appreciating, or increasing, in value.* In other words, if you're making installment payments on a car, a washing machine or other items that go down in value each year, then you're not using credit wisely.

If your total credit payments each month (not includ-ing house payments) do not exceed *about 5 percent of your net spendable income* (the income you have left after subtracting taxes, a tithe or fixed percentage for charitable gifts, and a percentage of your gross income that you allot to a basic investment program), then you're fairly safe. But in these uncertain economic times, when we are plummeting into an eventual currency collapse, I recommend that my clients unload all the debt obli-gations they can, as soon as they can. The reason this approach is so radical is that the majority of advisers tell their clients to borrow heavily and pay it back with "cheaper" dollars. The problem is, what if you get caught without those cheaper dollars and lose a lifetime of effort in one month?

What are my reasons for this rather extraordinary posi-tion in our credit-crazy society? First of all, families who lose their jobs during a major currency crisis will have enough trouble just paying for food and shelter, and cer-tainly won't need creditors knocking on their doors every day. In fact, even a nominal amount of debt during a crisis can escalate into dire problems if a family has to go for many months without a regular income.

But there's another reason for getting completely out of debt that has direct application to your financial power right now, before any collapse occurs. If you're constantly getting into difficulties with excessive credit, the tendency is to become preoccupied with those problems and to neglect other important areas of your financial plan. Many people have lost all their flexibility because all their potential surplus is going into old debts. The best way to avoid this situation is to get completely out of debt and stay out. And I'll put this in even stronger terms: *Your number-one financial goal should be to become debt free.*

In our society, three factors have emerged as the biggest culprits in leading us into debt, and you should avoid each one of them. Here they are:

Credit cards. You've probably heard other financial counselors say that the first thing they do when a family is having budget problems is to direct them to destroy all their credit cards. That may seem like an extreme solution, but I agree with it entirely.

At the same time, though, I'm not unalterably opposed to credit cards. Sometimes, it's important in business to have records of restaurant costs or other purchases for tax purposes, and a credit card is a convenient way to accumulate accurate records. Also, if you need to rent a car, it's very difficult to do so in this country without some sort of national credit card.

But in general, I advise those who have even the slightest tendency to misuse credit cards to prove the practicality of this idea by trying to go without plastic money for a while. I eliminated my credit cards several years ago—

134

even though I never had any problems personally with them. I counseled many others to live without credit because they couldn't manage it, and inevitably they would ask, "What about you? Do *you* use credit cards?" If I had to answer yes, that would undercut the counseling I was giving them, so I decided to make a commitment to a cash-only existence. Through the use of traveler's checks and other noncredit means, I found that it is not only possible but immensely enjoyable to operate this way. Those who try it may well find they don't want to go back to the cards.

It's not the cards themselves but their *misuse* that has created such a financial mess for the average American. I've run across people who are able to use credit cards in such a way that they don't actually get into debt. But I've never met anybody who really uses them *wisely* for personal purposes because these cards prompt us to buy things that we would probably not buy if we had to use cash. In other words, they lead us down the dangerous road of impulse buying. Remember, people don't set out to get themselves so deeply into debt that they can't pay their bills. It always happens because of poor planning.

Automatic overdrafts. One of the most insidious credit traps that exist today is the automatic bank overdraft. This service, which is provided by many banks under a variety of names, such as "checking plus," allows a customer to write a check even if he or she doesn't have sufficient funds to cover it. The bank provides an automatic loan for the overdraft and conveniently adds interest until it is paid off.

This type of credit is insidious because it encourages families to be sloppy with their bookkeeping and tempts them to buy things they can't afford. Stay away from any system that encourages impulse buying and slothfulness.

Solomon said in Proverbs 27:23-24, "Be sure you know the condition of your flocks, give careful attention to your herds; for riches do not endure forever, and a crown is not secure for all generations."(NIV) Unfortunately, most people with these overdraft accounts aren't aware of the precise condition of their "flocks" and "herds."

Surety. Surety is most commonly thought of as cosigning for the debts of another person. Although cosigning is a form of surety (and a foolish one), it is not the only one. Surety can also mean taking on an obligation to pay without a certain means of repayment. Therefore, if you borrow money and sign a personal note to repay it should the collateral prove deficient, and you don't have other assets you've set aside to comfortably cover the debt, then you are in surety.

Black's Law Dictionary suggests the serious nature of this sort of obligation by defining a surety as one "who undertakes to pay money or to do any other act in event that his principal fails therein." In practical terms, if you cosign a bank note or other debt obligation for someone else, you may think you're just doing him a favor. But wait until you have to pay off the loan! You'll quickly find that not only do you owe an unexpected debt, but you have lost your friend as well.

In Proverbs 22:26, Solomon warns: "Be not one of those who give pledges, who become surety for debts. If you have nothing with which to pay, why should your bed be taken from under you?" (RSV) The same can be said for pledging yourself to pay off another person's loan, even if the loan is being set up as part of a "surefire" investment scheme. To do so, foolishly risks personal assets that may be demanded from you as payment for the loan obligation. This problem often arises in joint real estate investments, where someone "leverages" the property by buying it with a number of other investors for a small down payment and a large loan obligation and then personally endorses the note. Later, if the note cannot be paid and the property reverts to the lender, the lender can sue the borrower for any deficiencies and can literally come in and "remove his beds," as Solomon cautioned.

Our early American forebears took this principle of avoiding surety and other debt-inducing arrangements very seriously because the result of imprudence might be debtor's prison. For us, likewise, getting out of debt should be a premier goal in the process of setting up a crash-proof financial plan.

Principle Two: Arrange Your Finances So That You Can Generate a Surplus. This is where the bare-bones part of your budget really comes into effect because it will be necessary for you to evaluate every single area of your expenditures very closely so that you can cut back or eliminate waste. In this way, you'll have the best chance of generating some extra money that you can use in an investment strategy. This surplus goal applies to those with modest incomes as well as to those with large incomes. *Regular* savings is the key to financial security.

Why worry about creating a surplus? For one thing, you need a buffer to serve as a cushion that will protect you against the uncertain movements of the economy. If you're spending every last cent of your income, then you lack any such cushion in case of even a minor economic setback or personal financial calamity. But if you have been able to accumulate a savings or investment cushion with your surplus, you'll be much better prepared to weather any economic storm.

The second reason to create a surplus is to provide extra funds for investments. There are extensive discussions later in this book on ways you can increase your net worth dramatically with virtually crash-proof investments, even in hard times. But without any extra money on hand, your options are severely limited.

Finally, perhaps the most important reason to create a surplus is to enable you to give more away to others through the community programs of your choice.

Principle Three: Having a Debt-Free Home Should Be One of Your Primary Financial Goals. If you're like most homeowners, you probably did a double take when you read this principle. After all, the common wisdom is that it's always best to have a mortgage on your home so that you can take advantage of interest write-offs on your tax returns.

But I take issue with this common advice. In the first place, it's relatively *recent* common advice. As mentioned earlier, during the 1920's nearly everybody in the United States owned his home debt free. But today, nearly everyone leases a home with a mortgage attached. In other words, we've shifted from a principle of outright home ownership to a principle of home leasing through indebtedness. Not only has this trend placed the average American family in peril of losing its home, but it has also driven the cost of homes out of the range of the average family's income. Any sizable financial crisis will find most families unable to make their house payments.

There's a tendency these days to look at people who redirect their assets toward paying off their home as a little "odd." On the contrary, the person who works to own his or her own home is one of the wisest among us. The simple truth is, a mortgaged home is always in jeopardy of being repossessed. It only takes an occurrence only a matter of the right (or wrong) economic conditions. A debt-free home represents economic security.

In our high-inflation economy, why should you want to pay off your home? And what about the loss of your tax deductions for mortgage payments? First of all, nobody ever made any money by paying out interest to a bank, and especially not at the exorbitantly high rates lending institutions now charge. The only way you can make money on a mortgage, except through whatever equity increase you may get on the underlying property, is to put the money that might go for a house purchase into income-producing investments that can earn more than the interest paid on the mortgage. That's hard for most people to do consistently, and it still leaves the home in jeopardy. For example, what happens if the investment income dries up?

Even if you're in a 50 percent tax bracket, you still end up paying out more than you take in with a mortgage. In other words, in a 50 percent bracket, if you give the mortgage company one dollar, at most you'll get back fifty cents from the IRS through deductions, but you've still lost fifty cents.

But there's an even more important consideration in favor of paying off a home as soon as possible. The way I like to pose this issue is to ask, "Do you plan on living in your home for the rest of your life, or at least for a fairly long period of time? Or are your mortgage outlays just payments in lieu of rent?"

To put it another way, would you be absolutely devastated if you lost your home in a currency crisis, during which you couldn't meet the monthly mortgage payments? Or would you look upon the loss of your home the way you would view a failure to make rent payments?

What I'm getting at is this: It seems to me that many investment counselors have made far too much of the home as an investment. In most cases, people don't regard their home as an investment at all. They regard it as a *purchase*. In other words, they don't ever expect to sell it, realize a profit and then put the money into some other investment. If they sell it at all, it will only be to buy another home which will give them a roof over their heads but won't put an extra penny in their pockets—at least not in the foreseeable future.

So people who buy a home as a purchase are much like those who buy jewelry to wear and enjoy, rather than to trade as a commodity. I had one man ask me, "Do you know a place where I can buy a diamond?"

I replied, "Yes, I have a good friend who is a principal buyer for one of the diamond firms in South Africa. He can get you a very good deal on a fine diamond. But why do you want it?"

"I want it as an investment, but I want it mounted in a ring for my wife to wear," the man said.

"Then you don't want to buy an investment-grade stone," I told him.

"Yes, I do want it as an investment," he insisted.

"No, you want it as a *purchase*," I said. "How much

trouble do you think you'd have getting that ring off your wife's finger to sell it?"

"I don't know," he admitted.

"And how many other things would she want to sell before she got rid of that diamond?"

"Virtually everything," he said, and then the light began to dawn. It was obvious that he wanted a diamond because it would be something that would please him and his wife, not because they were thinking in terms of a good investment.

And for many people, it's much the same way with a home. A home is the last thing many families would want to release when the time came to reevaluate and reorder an investment portfolio. So I usually don't even include the home in a portfolio, though it would obviously be a part of the family's total net worth.

Also, having the security of a place to live, even if you're without a regular job, is an almost immeasurable psychological advantage in hard times. I counsel many professional athletes, who have quite high incomes for a short number of years and then often have very little coming in during the transition period between leaving their sport and finding a regular job. One of the first goals we encourage is to pay off their homes.

Many of their tax attorneys and accountants disagree with this advice, pointing out the usual tax-write-off arguments of a mortgage. But these athletes and particularly their wives have a much more solid foundation to operate from when they know they have a place to live. The knowledge that their families are secure in a debt-free home has gone a long way toward reducing marital tensions and heading off potential divorces.

If you have your house paid for, there's an implicit

assumption in the back of your mind that says, "No matter what happens to my job, the American currency or whatever, nobody can come and take my home."

For anybody more than fifty years old, I would suggest that in *any* circumstance owning your own home outright should be one of your top personal financial goals. If a younger person loses his job or otherwise faces tough economic times, he has some years to recoup and bounce back. But those fifty and older are running out of time for their most productive efforts, and they need to be more cautious.

Underlying this advice about owning your home debt free is an assumption that the rules of investing have changed markedly over the last twenty years. Two decades ago, we saw only growth as we looked ahead into the future. But now, we have to be concerned about economic survival as well as growth. We have been through the credit-growth period in our economy. Now we must either restrict credit severely or face runaway inflation—and either alternative is going to spell trouble for many unwary American families.

I often think of this change in outlook in terms of a person who is paddling down a river in a canoe. Twenty years ago, you may have gotten ahead of the stream or perhaps fallen behind sometimes, but you always knew the direction was straight ahead. In other words, your investments may have done better or worse than the economy as a whole, but economic growth was the order of the day.

But today, the course of the river has changed. The water is moving along faster, and there's an uneasy sound we keep hearing—a sound that any experienced oarsman will recognize as a waterfall. We're still paddling in the same direction, but we have to keep a careful eye out for that waterfall—that currency collapse—or our journey may end abruptly and disastrously. But if we can take advantage of the speed of the current, and then get out of the water before we go over the edge, and walk around to the calmer streams below, we'll be a lot farther ahead than if we have to try to recover from a crash landing.

The practical fact is this: The investments that worked twenty years ago, when inflation was low and money was cheap, just won't work today. Living on borrowed money has proven to be living on borrowed time. And that's why those who can should *own* their home, not owe for it.

So if you decide to follow this piece of advice, how do you go about it? Certainly it takes more than just saying, "Okay, now I'm going to pay off my home." It will require a major financial commitment over a period of several years for most people.

Not everybody has the financial capacity to pay off a home, and for those people, I'd just say, don't worry about what you can't do. Concentrate on what you *can* do. If you can't pay off your house, pay off your car. Start somewhere! Once your car is paid for, use the freed money to pay on your mortgage.

But if you're one of those fortunate people who has the additional financial capacity to pay off your home, here's the sort of approach you might use:

Assume a family bought a home for $130,000 and arranged to finance it over thirty years at a 12 percent interest rate.

At the end of thirty years, if they make the regular mortgage payments over the entire period, they will have paid back about $350,000 at this rate. This will mean the average yearly payments on this house will be about $11,700, or approximately $970 a month.

But now, suppose they chose to pay the home off more quickly than the mortgage rate requires by accelerating the principal payments. Each month they could pay both the regular mortgage payment and *also* the principal due on the next month's payment. On the house in our example, that would amount to about $60 to $70 extra each month the first year, or a monthly payment that would increase from about $970 to $1,030. As the years pass, the amount paid on the principal would increase and the interest payments would decline. Obviously, the total payments would increase each year, but most people find that their ability to pay more also increases proportionally, so it shouldn't create a financial strain if they were living on a good budget plan.

By following this method consistently, they could completely pay off their mortgage in ten years instead of thirty —and would have trimmed about $150,000 off the interest payments. In other words, the home would ultimately cost $200,000 instead of $350,000.

Principle Four: Husbands and Wives Should Communicate Regularly About Their Long-Term Financial Goals. Like almost every other principle that governs the underground economy, this one has roots deep in our past—and it's about as old-fashioned a notion as you can find. In fact, it's founded on the belief of many of our ancestors that God made a husband and wife to function as "one" in a marriage.

One of the earliest references to the importance of the wife's role in family finances is expressed in Proverbs 31.

144

There, the "good wife," or the "wife of noble character," as different translations describe her, is an expert in financial affairs, managing her household, overseeing the family's charitable donations and apparently operating a business quite successfully. Now, as well as then, both spouses are essential to a well-balanced financial plan. I personally believe God puts opposites together because otherwise, one of them would be unnecessary. Husband and wife are almost always different, but one should never be regarded as inferior to the other in household management. Unfortunately, most wives play a very small role in the family's financial decisions—hence the mess we're in.

The wife's role in many early American families was similar to the Hebrew model, as she had vast economic responsibilities while working shoulder to shoulder with her husband on the family farm or helping him run the small family business in town. In many ways, they were equal partners in managing their personal finances, and if the husband or wife died, the survivor was experienced enough to continue successfully.

This teamwork concept, in which the wife shared directly in the work and decision making that shaped the family financial fortunes, was described by the Frenchman Alexis de Tocqueville, who traveled across the United States in 1831: "The same strength of purpose which the young wives of America display in bending themselves at once and without repining to the austere duties of their new condition, is no less manifest in all the great trials of their lives. In no country in the world are private fortunes more precarious than in the United States. It is not uncommon for the same man in the course of his life to rise and sink again through all the grades that lead from opulence to poverty. American women support these vicissitudes with calm and unquenchable energy; it would seem that their desires contract as easily as they expand with their fortunes."

But then a shift seems to have taken place in the last part of the nineteenth and early twentieth centuries in many American homes. The husband often assumed all the financial responsibilities of the home as well as his business, and in many cases he put his wife on an allowance. She frequently knew little or nothing about the overall financial workings of the home because the husband handled much of the bill paying and all of the investments. And when their husbands died, many of these women were totally helpless at first in trying to make some sense out of the family estate.

Then, still another disastrous change occurred in many American homes during the 1930's and in later years. With the husband in charge of the household finances and investing, increasing numbers of families began to follow the lead of the federal government in borrowing heavily and living on credit. As American affluence grew and family financial dealings became more complex, the man of the house began to lose control over the household financial situation. He didn't have time to oversee both his business affairs and his family finances with sufficient care, and the first thing that suffered was the household.

What we need to do now is to return to the original financial partnership that existed between many husbands and wives prior to our "enlightened" generation. That means recognizing that husband and wife always have different skills simply because they are different people.

You and your spouse need to plan a time alone to discuss both the budget and longer-term financial goals. Use some self evaluation: Are you really in control of your personal finances, or are they in control of you? What do you as a couple want to achieve with your money? Don't wait until you're ready to retire to discover that you've been following the wrong retirement program! Or if you keep getting a thought at the back of your mind that you should be giving more away to community service activities, or your church or some other charity, discuss it together and then commit yourselves to doing it. Good marriages, like good business partnerships, flourish in the financial area when both parties feel free to express their ideas and opinions—and to disagree when something strikes either as being wrong. Seldom will two opposites totally agree on a major decision, but if each respects the other's position, the result will be better than if only one person is working on the problem.

I recall a situation I once faced in counseling a husband and wife. The husband was describing a get-rich-quick scheme he had become fascinated with, and I heard him out on it. Then I turned to his wife and asked, "What do you think about what your husband is saying?"

"I don't know what he's talking about," she replied. "But it sure doesn't give me a feeling of peace."

I *did* know what he was talking about, and it amazed me that with a total lack of facts, she had come to the right conclusion—because what her husband wanted to get into was absolute nonsense and would have resulted in a financial disaster.

Both husband and wife should get into a *permanent* financial relationship and should share all things in common, particularly financial affairs. Too often, a man or woman enters a marriage with unrealistic expectations. The result of expecting too much or sharing too little is, in too many cases, divorce. It takes time, understanding and calm, rational planning over several years to develop a good mutual management system for personal finances. Eventually, one or the other partner will gravitate naturally toward the role of bookkeeper and financial manager. As each learns to appreciate the other's strengths and to discuss difficult issues rationally, the family's total financial picture will be enhanced in ways neither spouse could achieve operating alone.

To fully appreciate the vitality of the underground economy, it's absolutely necessary for husband and wife to learn to operate as a team. Not all of our early American ancestors achieved this goal, but many had more time to learn to work together as can be seen by the fact that their marriage records were much better than ours. Also, they lived in a simpler society which had such helpful economic support features as minimum government interference and community self-help programs.

It's not easy to find good models of the husband-wife economic team these days, but as the economy gets worse, more people will have to develop these skills.

Principle Five: Don't Worry About Things You Can't Do. One of the things that's always bothered me most about many of the popular economic doomsday books is that they suggest changes that in practice are impossible because of financial or time limitations.

For example, if you have to buy a well-equipped farm out in the woods, lay up a tremendous hoard of food, ammunition and other supplies, and also stock up on plenty of silver and gold, where are you going to get enough money to survive *until* the crisis occurs? Possibly, some of the suggestions made here may be equally out of reach of some readers. As a result, they have been arranged so that they can be implemented in stages, according to the economic capacity of each individual. Also these changes are applicable to those with typical life-styles at a variety of income levels and are useful in the present economy, regardless of whether or not there's a currency collapse.

We've covered a lot of ground up to this point, but before we go any further, take a moment to reflect on the main issue: How can you lose if you manage to become debt free, improve financial communications in your marriage and generate a surplus of money through a well-organized family budget? You'll come out ahead whether there's a monetary crisis or not. And suppose you can also succeed in paying off your home so that you and your spouse will *know* that, regardless of what happens, you'll have a roof over your heads. All that money now going into mortgage payments could then go into investments with a higher growth potential.

We cannot solve our economic problems; the best we can do is delay the inevitable. Yet I believe in the principles I present, and I've put each of them at the top of my own personal financial plan. But we need more than just principles. We also need a plan of action to implement them. Now let's take a closer look at where your money *is* going, and where it *should* be going, as you prepare to work and invest in the underground economy.

CHAPTER TEN

How to Create More Money

Now, let's discuss exactly how you can establish a budget in your own home that will allow you to generate a surplus of funds on the income you're making right now.

The use of a budget doesn't mean you have to live at the subsistence level in order to establish a surplus to invest. It does mean that your main goal should be to eliminate all waste and uncontrolled expenditures that sap your potential to invest. Just the "miscellaneous" expenses in your family finances cause hundreds, even thousands, of dollars to slip through your fingers each year. It's these expenses that have to be pared down to the bare bones of what you really need, rather than what you desire. This approach to family financial management requires that you cease impulse buying and learn to treat the first dollar as carefully as the last.

There are three basic steps you'll find helpful to follow in establishing a workable family budget. It's important to take each step in sequence to ensure that the budget you wind up with is the best plan for *your* family and not someone else's.

Step One: Find Out Where Your Money Is Going. Most people don't have the slightest idea how much they're actually spending, month by month, and they usually don't worry about it unless they end up in a financial mess and creditors get into the act.

The best way of determining your actual expenditures is to keep a *sixty-day diary* of every penny you spend. Don't change your habits during this period—just record every outlay for candy bars, newspapers, groceries, soft drinks or whatever. The discipline of this exercise will likely be the hardest thing you ever do in setting up a budget. So don't assume, just because the budget process starts out by requiring you to keep detailed records, that you'll have to continue it forever: You won't! It's only necessary to determine your present spending levels.

Step Two: Settle on an Appropriate Life-style for Yourself and Your Family. This can be a rather revealing exercise that demonstrates that husband and wife are different, but that different does not necessarily mean inferior. Also, these discussions can develop better financial communications between you and your spouse—and your children as well.

One of the best ways to go about this is to set aside a couple of hours one afternoon or evening, when you least expect to be interrupted. Discuss each area of the budget, such as housing, cars and food outlays. Also, you should discuss vacations, insurance and everything else that is necessary to enable you to make personal financial decisions. It's also a good idea at this point to list these items and activities in order of their priority in your family's life. For example, if regular vacations in Florida are more important than gourmet foods, you should indicate that fact.

It's also important to identify those money outlays that you regard as *absolutely necessary* to a decent life—such as your basic housing and food costs. (You can indicate the luxury items at this time.) Jot these necessities down in a separate category where you can refer to them later in our budget exercise.

Step Three: Set Up Your Basic Family Budget. This is the heart of any financial plan and requires both discipline and determination. It *must* be a plan made by both husband and wife—together. Also, it must be realistic and based on the best plan for *your* finances and not someone else's.

First of all, let me give you some encouragement about the value of the time spent to develop this system. One of the main reasons that many families shy away from a budget is an unrealistic idea of the time required. *Any* plan requires some effort and time, but if it necessitates a disproportionate amount, you have the wrong plan.

Initially, it will take a couple of hours to discuss and write down your goals and objectives. Then, you can count on a couple more hours to write out the budget. Finally, it will take about *half an hour a week* to maintain it. This is a small price to pay for financial peace of mind and harmony in a critical family area. I have counseled hundreds of families who found the effort demanded in establishing a budget both enjoyable and rewarding—and I believe the same experience can be true for you as well.

Finally, you can't hope to plan for the future unless you have a plan for today.

Now let's examine the steps necessary to set up a sound budget: You can see from your diary how much you spend each month, and thus you will know the general areas that need to be controlled or eliminated. The first step in the budget process is to list your total income each year. Include *everything*: salaries, moonlighting fees, investment income, honorariums, annual gifts you get regularly from other family members, and so on. Now add these figures to get your gross annual income. Let's suppose, for purposes of this discussion, that after you've added up everything you earned last year, you find you have a gross annual income of about $37,000.

The next step is to subtract three key items from your gross income. These consist of taxes, regular charitable gifts (such as tithes and offerings to your church) and a minimum percentage of your gross income that you want to invest each year.

Obviously, taxes are listed as a top priority because the government takes its portion first. In reality, however, taxes should be last because they can be controlled by proper charitable giving and "tax-wise" investing. Unfortunately, most people neither give nor save—with the result that they end up with nothing or only a minimal amount each year after taxes and expenses. The result is that the average sixty-five-year-old man has less than $1,000 in assets.

It's for the very reason that gifts and investments get squeezed out that I've put them first. They are of prime importance as you organize your personal budget.

For the three priority items—taxes, charitable gifts and

investments—it's important to get the money alloted to them out of your hands *immediately.* The principle is simple: If the money allocated to the priority items is no longer available, you'll have no choice but to learn to live on what's left. This approach to priority items is what might be called "budgeting off the top." The government has used it quite effectively to get its money first through withholding tax. If you take a similar approach, all you have to worry about is dividing up the money that remains among those expense categories that have a lower priority in your financial plan.

I suggest that my clients contribute a tithe, or 10 percent, of their gross income to what they regard as God's work through the qualified charitable organizations of their choice. Then, I recommend that they take another 10 percent from their gross income for the investment surplus. Finally, after taxes are subtracted, the amount left is called the *net spendable income.* It's that amount that will be allocated to cover the basic living expenses.

For example, if your gross annual income is $37,000, you might subtract about 15 percent for your taxes, or $5,550. Then you would take out 10 percent of your gross for charitable gifts, or about $3,700. Finally, another 10 percent, or $3,700, would come out for your investments. The total of these three subtractions would come to just under $13,000, and that would leave you with a net spendable income of approximately $24,000.

This net spendable income represents the actual amount of income available for your regular household operating expenses. I always find it necessary to make one final calculation and that is to divide the annual figure by twelve to find out how much money is available to a family each month. So, in our example, you would divide the $24,000 by twelve and find you have $2,000 net spendable income to live on each month. The next logical question is how should that $24,000 be divided up?

There's one underlying principle that always has to be respected, no matter how many expense categories you may have and what percentage of your net spendable income you assign to each of them: *The absolute requirement is that the total amount spent can't exceed 100 percent of your income!* If you spend more than 100 percent, as many families do, then, like the federal government, you're going to find yourself getting deeper and deeper in debt. And like a house built upon sand, your household finances will come tumbling down during the first windstorm.

Here are some guidelines on expense categories and typical percentages of net spendable income that will work for families with spendable incomes of $4,000 a month or less. They will also work for higher incomes when spending is *limited* to $4,000 or less.

Housing: You should spend no more than 35 percent to 40 percent of your net spendable income on all housing-related costs, including mortgage or rent, taxes, utilities, maintenance, telephone and various forms of housing insurance.

For example, with a net of $24,000 annually, you would limit yourself to an absolute maximum of $9,600 a year or $800 a month. This may seem like a lot of money, but remember: We're talking about your *total* housing-related expenditures. When you start adding in telephone bills, general maintenance costs and other peripheral items, you may well find that $800 a month isn't really as much as you thought.

If you have a particularly attractive apartment or home that you want but it costs you 50 percent of your net, then you have to make a decision: Either you give it up and find a place that fits in the recommended percentages, or you take that extra 10 percent out of one or more of the other expense categories we'll discuss. Unfortunately, it's not simple to cut back any of the percentages because none are extravagant.

I have had people say, "But I like this house—it's just not fair that I should have to give it up and get a cheaper place!" Obviously, the choice is theirs, not mine. But no matter what I may say or they may think, there is still only 100 percent of income available to spend without going into debt.

And let me offer a little aside at this point: If you decide early in your money management program that you want to pay off your home quickly, as I suggested in the last chapter, you'll find that your housing costs will drop dramatically after you send in that last mortgage check. Also, you'll have much more flexibility in your over-all budget either to invest or to give away.

Food: Our hypothetical family can afford to spend 15 percent of their net on food—and that means food prepared at home, not meals bought in restaurants. In other words, with $24,000 a year or $2,000 a month in cash, they would be limited to $300 a month for home-cooked meals.

You may find you can get along on slightly less than 15 percent or you may have to spend a little more, depending on your family's appetite and the cost of food in your particular part of the country. But if your food budget rises too far over this percentage, you'll find yourself having a lot of trouble keeping your total expenses within 100 percent of your total net spendable income.

Car and transportation: Allocate about 15 percent of your net spendable income to this category, which in cludes your car maintenance, insurance, installment payments, gas and oil and every other outlay related to the automobile. Also, if you live in a city like New York, where you may often find yourself using cabs, buses and subways to get around, you have to figure those costs in this category, too.

Insurance: The fourth category in your budget is insurance. This should consume about 5 percent of your net spendable income. Health and life insurance needs are included here; insurance payments related to automobiles and housing would go under those separate categories.

If you don't have access to group insurance rates, your payment percentage may jump to as much as 7.5 percent, but don't let it rise beyond that. Otherwise, you're likely to become what has popularly been called "insurance poor." Insurance is meant to provide for *logical* future needs, not illogical ones.

A word of warning is necessary here: Never fall into the trap of looking on any insurance policy as a form of investment. Accept your insurance expense as just that—an expense. Purchase the amount and type that fits *your* need, not an insurance agent's need to sell. Learn to buy insurance rather than be sold it!

But how much life insurance does your family need? A detailed discussion of this subject is beyond the scope of our book, but let me offer a few general comments. Many insurance salesmen picture the need for life insurance in terms of a bell-shaped curve, where you need less as a young couple, the most when your income is at its peak in middle age and then less when you get older.

But I don't agree with that. The young family with several young children needs the most protection, and the need for insurance drops off regularly as the children get older and savings and investments increase. The main idea in determining the right amount of insurance is to figure how much either surviving spouse would need, in the eventuality of the other's death. This should include such things as child care, education and possible relocation. Then you should purchase the amount of insurance dictated by your need. The budget percentage will help to determine the type of insurance. Most couples I counsel select annual renewable term insurance because it affords the most protection at the least cost during the children's growth years.

Our model family with $2,000 net spendable income monthly might be able to afford 5 percent, or $100, for insurance each month. If they need more, then they either have to subtract the extra amount from some other budget category, find a less costly type of insurance or just resolve to get along on less insurance.

Debts: The amount of money you put into servicing interest and principal on debts each month should be limited to no more than 5 percent of your net.

Debt in this context does not include any mortgage you may have on your home, because that should come under the budget allocation for housing. Also exclude payments you make to buy a car because, once again, this amount would be included under your car and transportation expenses.

But this category does encompass all credit card purchases and installment payments on things like household appliances. If a family commits a greater amount to miscellaneous debts, they are eating into funds that should be allocated to investments, charitable gifts or family needs.

Some people, of course, don't have to worry about this category. One man came in to see me about his personal financial program and when he noticed that 5 percent debt category, he said, "That's stupid! I'm not going to give somebody 5 percent of my income! I don't owe anybody else a cent, and you're telling me I've got to go out and borrow money and pay interest to somebody?"

I explained, of course, that it was perfectly all right for him to continue to operate without debt. In fact, I recommend that every couple get completely out of debt if possible. But, I told this man, some people will always have some debts just because of the life-style they've chosen, and for them a limit of 5 percent is a sacrifice.

As a matter of fact, to many people a limit of 5 percent for debt service appears nearly impossible. Many families I counsel are paying 15 percent to 25 percent of their net spendable income to their creditors. No family can maintain that rate for very long and hope to meet other household expenses. Soon they must borrow just to make payments on money they owe.

So if you find, after putting together your sixty-day budget diary, that you're paying out more than 5 percent to creditors, you should seriously consider going on a crash program to retire those excess debts as soon as possible. Get rid of your credit cards and resolve to live without borrowing. Then, after you've set up your Bare-Bones Budget, take every cent of surplus you set aside and apply it immediately to paying off those loans and other obligations you've accumulated.

If you didn't get into debt in just three months, don't expect to get out of debt in three months. It will take time and some sacrifice, but it's worth it. Generally, most families can accomplish a debt-free goal in eighteen months. If you're in a heavy debt situation, the most important goal to shoot for is a complete retirement of all outstanding obligations as soon as possible. When you achieve this goal, you'll be in a much stronger position, not only to conduct your present financial affairs but also to weather any economic storms that may accompany a future currency collapse.

Entertainment and recreation: This sixth category of your budget should amount to approximately 7 percent of your net and will include vacations, trips, movies and eating out, among other things.

For those with a net spendable income of $24,000 a year, this represents only $1,700, or about $140 per month —not a very large sum to cover all the restaurant meals, movies, Little League equipment and vacation costs for a family of four. Unfortunately, through the use of credit cards, many families spend money far and above what they can actually afford. And they end up getting far into debt—usually just after a particularly extravagant vacation.

One couple came in to see me about a problem with excessive debts, and as we ran down their expenditures, we stopped for quite a while on this recreation category. I asked how much they spent a year just on vacations, and the husband replied, "Oh, about three hundred dollars a year."

But the wife said, "Now, honey, we spend more than that!"

So the husband upped the ante: "Okay, maybe five hundred dollars."

But the wife chimed in again, "Now, honey . . ."

By the time we had gone through three or four more "honeys," they were up to the actual amount they spent on vacations each year—about $1,300. They happened to have a net spendable income close to our hypothetical couple, so that meant they only had about another $400 to spend on the family's entire recreation program during the rest of the year. Of course, they spent much more than that, and their resulting indebtedness caused even greater problems.

I pointed out to this family that in order to take the kind of vacations they liked, they would have to set aside another $100 a month in a special savings account. They responded, "Oh, we can't afford that!" They were exactly right, and that meant they couldn't afford those vacations, either.

Clothing: This seventh category of your budget should take about 5 percent of the net income. Unfortunately, with growing children it doesn't take long to go through the $100 a month allocated here. But as we've already seen, by using such underground economy measures as the swap shop, you can reduce *clothing expenses substantially.*

Savings: This savings account, which should be about 5 percent of your net spendable income, is not the same as the investment surplus listed earlier as one of the three priority expenses. This account is for unexpected contingencies, like the deductible you might have to pay on a medical bill before your insurance goes into effect, or the repair bill you get when your refrigerator breaks down.

But there's a difference between this expense category and the others because in this case you want to accumulate only the maximum amount of money that would equal 5 percent of your annual net. In other words, with a net of $24,000, you would save up to $1,200 and then stop putting money into this account. If your savings dip below 5 percent of your annual net, however, you'd start replenishing the fund by contributing to it from your monthly income.

Some families also like to have a contingency fund like this to help other people who suddenly face financial need. In that case, it's good to know you have a little extra on hand to help them out.

Medical and dental: I advise my clients to set aside about 3 percent of their net for these expenses—and you should note here that health insurance isn't included under this category. It goes under the general insurance section.

If you have a particularly high deductible on your insurance and you confront extra medical expenses one year, then, of course, you would probably find yourself paying more than 3 percent, and you'd have to cut back on one of the other expense categories to stay under your total of 100 percent.

Miscellaneous: About 5 percent of your net should be going into this category, which might include newspapers, candy bars and anything else you can't conveniently place under the other expense areas. One couple with a small child asked me about diapers and other items they buy in the drug store, and I suggested they would probably want to include those things here—but it would probably mean they would need to increase the percentage. Other items that would come under this heading would be cleaning bills, private school expenses and most nonmedical drug store items (like toothpaste).

This miscellaneous area is especially difficult for many families because they often find their money is dribbling away in small individual sums which at the end of the month add up to a huge total. Like entertainment and recreation, this area may quickly increase to 10 percent, 15 percent, 20 percent or even more of your net if you're not careful—and if it does, that means you're going to find yourself deep in debt trouble.

These, then, are the basic areas you'll want to consider as you set up your budget—and remember, they can't total more than 100 percent of your net spendable income. You'll note that the figures I've given you don't quite add up to 100 percent, but they are just guidelines. When you tailor these figures precisely to your own situation, you must be sure you stay within your available income. Otherwise, your planning will be crisis-oriented, rather than surplus-oriented.

You'll also discover you have to make some special adjustments if you have kids in college or in an expensive private school. But generally speaking, the above categories should serve as a solid basis for the budgets of most families. This is not the final step, however. Once you've set up your budget, it doesn't do you any good if you put it in a drawer and forget about it. The ultimate key to any system of financial management is how well you maintain it, and that's the next step.

Step Four: Maintain Your Budget. Each family should set up a budget for only one year. If you try to plan your daily expenses any farther into the future, you'll find you can't anticipate prices and income well enough to make it worth while. And when you have all your categories and percentages established, it's a good idea to have one person—the best bookkeeper—be in charge of maintaining the system.

I don't think it should take any more than thirty minutes a week to keep up this budget. But how can you expect to spend so little time with so many specific expense categories?

The basic plan is achieved by a *zero-base budget*, where each month you start with zero in each expense category. The monthly allocation is listed for each category as a *deposit* and all expenses are shown as *withdrawals*. The key to the budget is never to let the balance get below zero, and that includes monthly allocations you make for annual outlays such as insurance and auto maintenance.

One advantage to this approach is that you can see clearly throughout the month whether you're getting ahead of planned expenses such as food or recreation. If you're spending too much, then you have to begin to cut corners to have enough to make it to the end of the month.

An even simpler method that some families use is the *envelope system*. With this approach, you decide which of your expense categories can be conducted in cash each month, and then you manage your money through envelopes labeled for each one of those cash-expense categories. Each payday you insert the cash you've allotted to each category and pay the expenses directly out of the envelopes.

Even more than the zero-base budget system, this envelope method has the virtue of signaling to you when you're about to exceed your budget allocations: When you run out of money in any envelope, you must do without until the next pay period.

So you can see from these suggested maintenance techniques that it shouldn't take an excessive amount of time to maintain your budget once you've set it up. You don't have to keep track of every cent you spend, and you don't have to keep voluminous records. In fact, you don't have to keep any records at all!

All you have to do is deposit your money in your envelopes or enter the appropriate amounts on each of your zero-base budget sheets, and then pace your spending so that it matches your needs. And if you should find that you are so frugal that you can sometimes run a surplus in one or more of your expense categories, then put the extra money into your savings or investment accounts—or just give it away!

Step Five: Devise a Crisis Budget. After you've set up your regular budget—and perhaps found you have to cut back on some of your expenditures to keep from going further into debt—you may think you're already involved with a "crisis budget." But unfortunately that's not the case. Don't forget, we may well be facing a major currency collapse. And that event may force many families to cut back their expenses to an *absolute* minimum. The crisis that is an inconvenience to the well-planned family will be a disaster for the unaware family.

So it's wise to look over this budget you've drawn up and see just where you could cut or eliminate costs still further if you had to for a time. There are obviously certain expense categories that are fairly inflexible, such as your mortgage or rent payments. But there are other areas, like food or recreation, where you may have more leeway for cutting back.

Here are a few ideas that people have put into effect to keep their expenses lower, even in fairly good economic times. Some might fit into your own financial program:

• To keep your recreation-vacation expenses down, try house-swapping with people who live in other parts of the country or the world, where you think you might like to spend your holidays. This sort of arrangement can cut your hotel expenses to zero and may, in resort areas, reduce your total vacation outlays by more than half.

• Gifts are a big "recreation" expense item for many families, so what some families elect to do is to lay down a rule that all Christmas gifts and other presents must be *made* by the family member. In other words, they never shop for gifts at all. That means they are always able to add a very personal touch to their gifts and also save hundreds of dollars each year that they can put into other things.

• To save on food, rely as much as possible on sales-shopping by employing the Underground Pantry Principle.

❖   ❖   ❖

The possibilities of preparing for a crisis are far broader than this brief list, of course. The main purpose of this crisis budget concept is to encourage you to start thinking and anticipating what you *might* do if and when a currency crisis strikes. But perhaps the best kind of preparation for the future, whether there is a collapse or not, is to put as much of your surplus as possible into wise investments. So it's the special techniques of investing by using underground economy principles that we'll turn to next.

CHAPTER ELEVEN

Ten Keys to Successful Investment in the 1980's

Up to this point, we've concentrated on the ways you can use the underground economy to generate a surplus of money. But now the question is, how can you best put that surplus to work? Specifically, how can you turn today's small investment into tomorrow's nest egg—or even abundance?

It's not important to make money for its own sake. Money should only be a *by-product* of certain types of success. Although money does often go hand in hand with personal achievement and social freedom, the well-to-do may have more personal problems than anyone else. In fact, the pursuit of wealth is often the cause of their misery. Peace does not come through the accumulation of material possessions but rather by centering on spiritual and moral values.

There is also another side of wealth to be considered, and that's the principle of *stewardship*. A steward is a manager of another's property. Some of the most effective philanthropists have been motivated by the conviction that they hold all their abundance in trust for others. Many also believe that they have received their material blessings directly from God, and God expects them to use their holdings wisely, for the benefit of His work. This same idea can apply to anyone, rich or not: As stewards we should multiply the assets entrusted to us—not just for our own benefit but to be able to share with the needy as well. So to allow material assets to erode through bad management is a sign of slothfulness—and poor stewardship.

If you just sit on your extra funds or put them into relatively low-yielding savings accounts, they will vanish before your very eyes under the corrosive impact of inflation. The United States economy has always been a dynamic system, ever changing and constantly moving into uncharted waters. So those who remain immobile with their money are likely to find themselves holding an empty purse a few years hence.

Also, if you're one of those fortunate people who has a surplus, you'll find that your opportunity to help others increases proportionately with your growing assets—and that can be a source of tremendous joy and good will. For example, you may want to help your family achieve a greater degree of security in the event of a currency crisis —or your untimely death. In addition, you will be able to increase your giving through charitable organizations. And finally, in tough economic times you may want to share your resources with members of your economic self-help community who are not as prepared to build up an adequate surplus.

There are thus many reasons other than greed for developing and multiplying your surplus. But how do you go about it?

Through financial counseling of families with and without a surplus, I've had an opportunity to see firsthand an incredible variety of needs in personal finance. No single plan will fit everyone. But unfortunately, most investment counselors tend to lump everyone into one mold. Coincidentally, that mold often fits the investment salesman's need for income. Salesmen are great for advice about their particular area of expertise, but should never be used as overall financial counselors.

Now let's look at some specifics you can use in planning your investment strategy with a view toward growth and security. Even though each family's needs are different, there are certain common principles that can provide a solid foundation for nearly anyone. I've distilled these principles into the following ten basic investment guidelines. Study them and tailor them to your personal needs so that you can use them as practical tools in implementing your own investment program.

1. Formulate a clear-cut investment goal. No one should invest without having some ultimate purpose for the money clearly in mind. Successful investing usually presupposes some final use for your funds, in part because the goal dictates the nature of the investment plan you choose. If you are without a goal, it's likely you're also without a plan—and no plan almost always means haphazard, ineffective investment decisions.

There are at least six valid personal objectives for an investment program, any of which may stand alone or be combined with one or more of the other goals:

Retirement. The first investment objective, preparing for retirement, most often requires an investment of surplus funds from regular earnings. Usually, a retirement-oriented individual is not independently wealthy and needs the majority of available income to live on. Budgeting is required to be able to generate the needed surplus (perhaps by taking that 10 percent for investment out of gross income as we suggested in the budgeting chapters). This person's main focus now is on building up a nest egg for his or her later years.

If the individual has a fairly high current income, it may also be necessary to use some of the available surplus to invest in tax shelters. Growth with minimum or moderate risk is a characteristic of investments made for retirement.

Preservation of assets. This second objective may suit the couple who have inherited a sizable sum—say $100,000 or more—but who feel that they don't have a special gift for making money. They just want to be sure that their money maintains its value, even in an economy of double-digit inflation. In other words, they will want their $100,000 to be worth about $200,000 in ten years if we assume the inflation rate will cut the value of their investment in half in that time.

Their source of funds for investment would, of course, be the existing assets they want to preserve.

Education. Many families have become especially concerned about this third objective as the cost of college skyrockets. Unlike those who are merely trying to preserve

172

assets, the family with children's education in mind must think more in terms of risk. If they balk at taking some chances on multiplying their assets fairly rapidly, they may well be left with inadequate funds to cover school expenses.

For example, suppose a couple with three kids can set aside $3,000 a year for college. The first child will become a freshman in ten years, and the other two will follow close behind. If the couple put their money into a savings bank, they may have $50,000 at the end of that ten-year period, but inflation will probably have halved that amount to $25,000 of buying power at today's prices. That certainly won't be enough to get three kids through four years of college almost simultaneously!

The source of this education investment will be the 10 percent of gross income that the individual has decided to invest under our underground economy budgeting strategy.

Income. The couple entering retirement and looking for a maximum cash flow to live on will likely have this fourth objective. They'll use their existing assets for investment because all their current income is necessary to cover living expenses. They can't accept too much risk with their funds, but they can't be too conservative, either.

For example, they may invest their money at a 10 percent return and then use that income to live on. But if inflation eats away at their capital assets at a 10 percent annual rate, their underlying capital will only be worth half as much five years later. And the buying power of their income will also drop by half. So they have to think in terms of gradual growth as well as income.

Growth. Individuals with this fifth objective may have

no ultimate specific goal for their assets. Or they may have something very specific in mind, such as increasing their charitable contributions or buying a vacation home. In any case, they want to see their investments increase as fast as possible, and that means stressing risk more than do people with other objectives. The source of their funds will probably be the 10 percent investment amount they set aside out of each paycheck.

Tax shelter. This sixth and final objective is one of the most complex and needs a little more explanation in this introductory section. Those in a high income tax bracket may seek an investment not only because it offers income or growth of assets but also because it has the ability to protect or "shelter" the person's high earnings from a big tax bite.

If you're in the 50 percent tax bracket, you should put your surplus into capital gains investments or tax shelters, but not into things like interest-bearing accounts, which would require you to pay ordinary income tax on the returns.

The person whose earnings are lower and whose tax bracket is less may also want to examine tax shelters. But the tax burden isn't usually so burdensome that the entire investment strategy has to be designed with a heavy stress on tax shelters.

To illustrate the tax-shelter approach, let's look at an actual case involving one of my clients who put his money into a gas-drilling operation. He invested $10,000 and got $8,000 of his money back the very first year through an investment tax credit, depreciation deductions and other tax savings. The drilling company eventually hit gas, and

174

his portion of the well was valued at approximately $80,000 because of his share in the underlying gas reserves.

He could have continued to receive $3,000 to $4,000 per year for about twenty years as the gas was extracted and sold. Instead, he opted to give his interest in the well to a qualified charity and claim the value of his portion as a charitable deduction. As a result of this decision, he ended up with an additional $70,000 tax deduction on top of those already claimed. In a period of less than two years, he had turned a $10,000 investment into $40,000 in saved taxes and a $4,000-a-year contribution to charity—all through good investment planning. Now, that's what I would call stewardship!

Obviously, every investor's situation is different and the tax laws are very complex. But the practical fact is that the tax laws exist for our benefit and using them wisely is our prerogative. Most assuredly, the IRS does its part to collect all it can, but we need to help wean our government away from too much money.

One final note about tax shelters: You should *never* get into an investment solely for the tax benefits. Any good investment is eventually supposed to make money for you, not lose it. If you put your funds into a project without thought of some ultimate return, you're throwing your money away. Also, there are many so-called tax shelters that require excessive risk and sizable personal liability. Stay away from these and seek good counsel about every tax avoidance investment.

2. *Avoid personal liability.* Some get-rich-quick business schemes, as well as a number of tax-shelter arrangements,

are available only if you accept personal liability for a large debt. As a second guideline, *never* make yourself personally liable for any investment.

For example, many people have recently plunged into leasing operations, such as trucks or railroad cars, where they may put $10,000 into the venture and, with other investors, sign a $500,000 personal note on borrowed capital. By making the personal note, they may be able to take a $50,000 to $60,000 tax write-off, but at the same time, they can't take the deduction unless they become personally liable.

Usually, something in the back of their minds says, "This isn't very smart!" But then they listen to the salesman or promoter, who assures them the personal note is just a formality. They may be told that as a practical matter, nobody will ever come after them for the $500,000. And besides, if they fail to put their personal liability in writing, the IRS won't allow the tax deduction.

Don't be swayed by that kind of argument. I have counseled several people where the deal fell through and the bank came after the investors for the $500,000 loan. Obviously, the promoters were well protected personally and suddenly became hard to reach.

So avoid personal liability at all costs! This warning applies whether your investment involves a tax shelter or not. If you have any question about whether you're taking on personal liability, have your attorney insert an *exculpatory clause* in any contract you have to sign. This provision will explicitly relieve you of any personal liability if the investment goes sour.

A failure to avoid personal liability can result in financial ruin for you as well as tragedy for your entire family

—as can be seen in an actual situation that occurred in Atlanta during the mid-1970's.

There was a boom in Atlanta real estate during the early 1970's, and many people made fortunes through leverage, or borrowing heavily to buy as much property as they could. In a typical case, one person would form a partnership, buy some land and then sell it to another partnership for a profit. Then the second party would sell the land to a third partnership or individual for a still higher price. So the land kept changing hands, and each time the new buyer would sign a personal note, unknowingly making all his other assets liable for payment of the real estate loan.

This auction atmosphere continued until land in the area was unrealistically priced above its actual utility value. Then disaster struck. In 1975, the Federal Reserve Board reduced the credit supply in an attempt to control inflation, which was then running at about 12 percent. The result was that sources of new buyers dried up as the credit dried up. The last buyers couldn't sell their land, nor could they meet the loan payments on their highly leveraged real estate. They had been gambling that they could make a few interest payments on the loan and then write those payments off against taxes. Finally, they would sell the property for a good profit before the payments of principal (which are not deductible) came due. But their expectations proved wrong.

So, one by one, they began to go bankrupt. Land which had been selling at $10,000 an acre couldn't be sold for $5,000. Hoping to hold onto something, the speculators sold their best properties first, at substantial discounts, just to get some cash to make payments. And a "musical chairs" effect started to occur, with the land passing back up the chain to previous buyers, none of whom were able to meet the loan payments but all of whom had signed personal notes.

Finally, the land ended up in the hands of the original owner who had no debt—and frequently that would be the farmer who had always lived closer than the speculators to the spirit of Shakespeare's warning, "Neither a borrower nor a lender be . . ."

Then, the lawsuits started. The first group of sellers sued the second on the basis of the personal liability note that had been signed. The second next sued the third, and so on, down the line. I counseled some of these people after they had become involved in this crisis, and I encountered hundreds of families—including individuals worth millions the year before—who now couldn't even hang onto their homes. They lost their cars, furniture, businesses and quite often even their personal belongings because everything they owned was covered by those personal notes they had signed.

These were people who a year earlier had said, "We can never lose in this investment. The price of land is bound to go up." But it didn't.

The lesson I derive from this incident and many others like it is that you should never buy an investment on the basis of a personal financial guarantee. If a person won't sell you property with a personal exculpatory clause in the agreement, that in effect means he doesn't think the property is worth what he's charging. In other words, he's unwilling to take your down payment and the property alone as collateral.

This is a conservative principle but found throughout

the book of Proverbs. It's called "surety." Surety means, in part, taking on a certain or sure obligation to pay without a certain way to pay it—except out of your entire personal assets. Only if an asset stands for its own liability do you have a certain way to pay—and that is to surrender the asset, and the asset only. (See Prov. 17:18.)

Undoubtedly there will be investments that you will have to pass up if you refuse to become personally liable. But ultimately you will be in a much stronger position because you will know what your actual assets are. If an asset can't stand for its own liability, you let it go—and thereby keep the rest of your estate intact.

3. *Evaluate your investments in terms of risk and return.* Whenever an investment opportunity comes your way, always step back for a moment and ask first, "Does the return I may get justify the risk I have to take?" Secondly, ask yourself, "Can I really afford to take this risk, given the assets I have on hand?"

As a general rule, the higher the return you expect, the more risk you'll have to face. For example, an oil-drilling investment involves high risk because the company you're backing may never strike oil. But if a well does come in, you may make a return of 1,000 percent or more a year on your investment.

If you expect a relatively low return, say less than 20 percent a year on your investment, your risk should also be low. Treasury bills, which are quite safe but offer a relatively low return per year, fit into this category.

With these guidelines in mind, if you expect a low return with a high risk, you'll know you're looking at a terrible investment. On the other hand, if you anticipate high returns with a relatively low risk, you may have found one of the best buys around.

4. Keep at least 50 percent of your investments debt free. This principle has been followed in practice for many centuries by wise financial men and women, and it's a principle I would heartily recommend to anyone today because it works. The basic idea is to use leverage or borrowed money (without personal liability!) in acquiring one half of your investments. But keep the other half of your holdings debt free. In this way, if you are unable to make loan payments because of a monetary crisis or other difficulty, you'll lose only half your assets. On the other hand, if a crisis never materializes and you can continue to make your payments, you'll have the potential for multiplying your assets more quickly on borrowed money.

But here's a word of caution: Even though it is feasible to borrow money on half your investments, avoid borrowing to finance daily living expenses, such as the purchase of clothes or appliances. There's a world of difference between these two types of credit. Loans to finance living expenses can never make you any money because the articles begin to depreciate immediately in value. On the other hand, if you borrow to make an investment which has a good chance of becoming an asset, you'll increase your personal worth.

5. Be patient. The smart investor should keep cash on hand only for emergencies. As a general rule, only 5 percent of your investments should be in cash or "near-cash" assets (bonds, bank certificates of deposit, etc.). In fact, usually the only good reason to have money in a liquid savings account or money-market fund is to have it available while you're looking for a good investment opportunity.

But even though it's important to get into a good investment as soon as possible, don't be hasty. Patience is one of the fruits of the Spirit which the Apostle Paul mentions in Galatians 5:22, and it's also a key quality for the wise investor. It's much easier to find a bad investment than a good one, and if you act too quickly, you may find you've made a drastic mistake. I often have to go through twenty-five bad investments before I find one good one. So take some time to study and reflect before you put your hard-earned money into anything, no matter how attractive it may seem at first glance. Remember that the get-rich-quick schemes always look the best initially. If they didn't, nobody would buy them.

6. Diversify. The old adage, "Don't put all your eggs in one basket," may apply to your investments more than to any other aspect of your life. Mutual funds, which hold a variety of common stocks, bonds or other types of assets, were founded on the principle that the small investor should have the protection of many different types of investments. In this way, if one or a few go bust, he won't lose all his assets. By buying a few shares of a mutual fund at a relatively low price, the investor can participate in the diversity of the entire fund, which may hold assets worth millions or even billions of dollars.

Now, I'm not enthusiastic about many types of mutual funds. But I do respect their commitment to diversification. So I would suggest that you split up your surplus money among several types of assets. In this way, if one investment tends to do well in one type of economy and another does well under other economic conditions, you'll have some protection no matter what happens.

One way to diversify is by placing your investments in different areas of the economy which tend to run counter to one another. For example, the prices of stocks and bonds often move in inverse proportion to one another. In an economy where inflation is rampant and interest rates are high, bonds will, generally speaking, be very low. If interest rates climb to 20 percent, those that you bought for $1,000 at a 9 percent return may only be worth $400. But a common stock may do the exact opposite and increase in value during an inflationary economy. Similarly, the value of real estate may move in an inverse relationship to the bond market.

But when the prices of stocks begin to drop rapidly, that's usually a sign that interest rates will come back down. The economy is cooling off, and investments like bonds may rise in value. So it's important to choose a variety of investments to give yourself a strong position, no matter what the economy may bring.

To make this point as personal as possible, assume you have $10,000 to invest. You might split the money down the middle, with $5,000 going into land, the other $5,000 into silver. The land will probably inflate with the general rate of inflation in a booming economy. Then, if there's a severe downturn, you may not be able to sell the land for a decent price, but your silver may well grow in value. With the next upturn in the economy, if you've held your land, you may find it's grown significantly in value.

It's important to remember, though, that the principle of diversifying investments does not involve a one-time decision. Rather, it's based on an ongoing series of decisions to buy and sell, and on an ability to maintain sufficient breadth and variety in the midst of this trading. A key to this investment strategy is to predetermine a point at which you will sell off your investments, either with a profit or a loss. It's nearly impossible to pick the exact peak or trough in an economic cycle. Many people try and end up losers. One of the most common errors in short-term investments such as stocks is to ride a loss too long, and thus accept too great a risk.

It's also important to diversify your portfolio by *risk*. In other words, you might think in terms of a multi-tiered portfolio, with five levels of investment possibilities: (1) secure income, (2) long-term income, (3) growth, (4) speculative growth, and (5) pure speculation.

Depending on your age, income and goals, you may choose to omit one or more of these risk levels as you pursue your diversification strategy. But it's still important to choose more than one risk area.

For example, if you're reasonably young and in a fairly high income bracket, you might downplay the current income level and concentrate on spreading your investments among the growth and speculative levels. Suppose you're a salesman, forty-two years of age, with a wife and three children, aged ten, fifteen and seventeen. Your annual income always exceeds $40,000, and you have $20,000 to invest right now, with the expectation of an additional $8,000 a year surplus to add to your personal capital. Your long-range goals are to provide for the education of your children, to buy some recreational property and to provide for your retirement.

You might put $4,000 into the first category, secure

INVESTMENT ANALYSIS

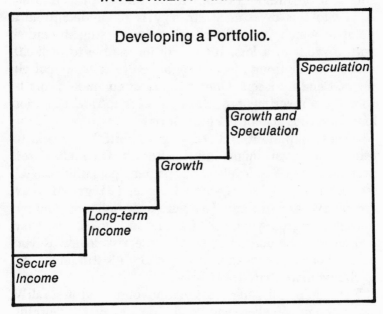

Developing a Portfolio.

Speculation

Growth and
Speculation

Growth

Long-term
Income

Secure
Income

Each level represents a degree of risk and de-
sired income or growth. The age, income and
goals of each investor will determine how much
(if any) should be invested in each category.

liquid income (perhaps a daily money-market fund), to cover emergency cash requirements. You'd skip the second category, long-term income, because you don't need that at your age and in your tax bracket. But then in the growth category you acquire $25,000 worth of leveraged beach lots, with a $6,000 down payment and a $100 monthly mortgage commitment. Another $5,000 might go into a speculative growth investment like a limited partnership that buys apartment buildings. And another $5,000 could be invested as pure speculation in gold or silver.

With this kind of portfolio—which is based on a real family's financial decisions—you would have achieved adequate diversification as far as the riskiness of your investments is concerned. Also, you would be protected by some economic diversification, with silver protecting you during an economic downturn, and real estate enabling you to take advantage of good economic conditions.

7. *Invest with an eye to long-range economic trends—especially the inflation rate.* General movements in the economy always have some effect on individual investments. So it's always important to think in terms of the national and local economies when you evaluate specific places to put your money. By taking this broader view of things, the investor is much more likely to know when to buy something when it's a bargain, at the lower end of its economic cycle, and when to sell it when it's near a peak.

It may seem obvious that you should buy low and sell high, but the typical investment philosophy *in practice* in America today is to buy high and sell low. Consequently, most people lose money in investments. The late financier

Bernard Baruch explained this strange phenomenon by pointing out that most people tend to get scared when their assets decline in value and they sell simply because they have failed to take a long-range view of things.

A key to successful investing is to have the courage to buy when other people are selling and then sell when they are buying. Don't let short-term trends or the herd instinct take control of your decision making. Baruch took the long-range approach, and he made billions of dollars as a result.

But of course, there's a little more to it than that. Even if you have some idea about where the national or local economy is headed, it won't do you much good unless you have studied how different investments react to different trends. For example, as we've already seen, land and newly issued bonds tend to soar in value during an inflationary, booming economy. Gold, on the other hand, often moves higher in economic downturns because bad times make people panic—and panic turns them to gold. This panic factor operates on a short-term basis and may result from the threat of war in the Mideast, the anticipation of an economic crisis or almost any other pessimistic news. But even aside from panic considerations, gold also tends to move up in value during a long-term economic growth cycle—as it has over the last twenty-five years.

Perhaps the most significant national trend that has affected and will continue to affect investments is inflation. In tracking ten different investments over the twelve-year period from 1969 to 1981, I discovered some interesting facts about their inherent growth potential and also about the impact inflation can have on different assets. Here is a summary of my findings in table form:

TEN KEYS TO SUCCESSFUL INVESTMENT

Asset	Value/ 1969	Value/ 1981		
			less inflation =	
Gold	$10,000	$55,000	*inflation =*	$22,000
Farmland	10,000	60,000	"	30,000
Silver	10,000	25,000		12,500
Apartments	10,000	42,857	"	21,429
Houses	10,000	30,000	"	15,000
U.S. Bonds	10,000	18,000	"	9,000
Commercial Paper	10,000	16,250	"	8,125
Savings Account (4.5%–6%)	10,000	14,599	"	7,299
Xerox	10,000	10,000	"	5,000
General Motors	10,000	10,000	"	5,000

As you can see from this list, the most *inflation-vulnerable* investments in recent years have been those like stocks, bonds, savings accounts, treasury bills and other fixed-income assets. Or to put it another way, they have failed to grow enough in value to offset the effects of inflation.

The most *inflation-proof* investments have been real assets that you can touch and use, like land and metals. In other words, they have appreciated sufficiently in an inflationary economy that their value, even after adjustment for inflation, has increased. There's certainly no guarantee that these trends will continue in the future for each of these specific assets. But there's no doubt in my mind that during the next five years, investors must take high inflation into account if they hope to place their money successfully.

8. *Focus on what you own outright, not on your "net worth" or total assets.* The term net worth doesn't refer to how much you own, but what your assets are above your liabilities. I know one man who literally bankrupted himself because of a concern to get rich quick and impress his friends. At one point, he was probably worth a quarter of a million dollars, with no liabilities. But then he began to expand his holdings so that he could own more than a million dollars worth of property and be able to say, "I'm a millionaire."

The problem that eventually brought him down was not net worth because his net worth soared to more than a million dollars fairly quickly. Unfortunately, though, his net worth actually represented $1.5 million in total value but also $.5 million in debt—and a portion of that debt encumbered each of his assets so that he didn't own a thing free and clear. He may have owned a lot of assets on paper, but they were all tied up in liabilities.

It didn't take a major economic downturn to wipe him out: A minor real estate downturn did it. He found himself unable to sell anything to generate cash, but he still had to make the payments on his debts.

9. *Before you buy, always know where you can sell.* This guideline is especially important when you're dealing

in "exotic" investments, like precious stones, silver or collectibles. Although these items can be excellent places to put your surplus, you can lose your shirt if you fail to educate yourself about outlets where you can sell when the market conditions are right.

For example, if you invest in silver, it's important to understand the difference between the retail and wholesale price, and to know where you as an individual dealer can get the best deal. The market price quoted in the newspaper and the street price that you can actually get for silver are often quite different. If you walk into a store with a silver plate and try to sell it over the counter, you may get only about $7 an ounce even though the *Wall Street Journal* quotes silver as being worth $14 an ounce. In order to get top dollar as an individual seller, you would have to present a pure silver bar to a reputable dealer. (Sterling silver plates and other kitchen utensils aren't pure and have to be melted down; the cost of that process lowers their market value.)

Or perhaps you are dealing in precious stones and are afraid if you turn a ruby ring in to be appraised, the gem dealer may replace it with a worthless stone. These and other fears and uncertainties can be largely eliminated if you deal only with recognized experts who are members of some professional organization, like the Gemological Institute of America. The key to successful investing in exotic items is to know your sources. Always buy from a legitimate broker who will guarantee to resell the item for you.

10. Every family member should be trained in the basic principles of sound investing. We've already talked about the role both husband and wife might play in household finances. More often than not, however, women who are more than willing to take over managing the household budget tend to take a back seat to their husbands when it comes to investments. Sometimes the wives may feel less qualified to oversee investments because their husbands are more involved in "business" matters at work, and investing seems very closely related to the businessman's stock in trade.

As often as not, this sort of attitude is way off base because the wife is just as capable of handling the investments as the husband. But even if the husband does take the lead in managing the family's capital accounts, it's a major mistake for the wife not to know something about the investment portfolio. If the husband dies before the wife acquires a working knowledge of the family's holdings, it could take her weeks, months or even years to sort things out after he's gone.

Children should also be brought into the family decisions about investing, both to make them more responsible when they inherit some of the family money and also to give them some training before they start to accumulate their own assets as adults. If you don't teach them, Sears, Roebuck or MasterCard will.

These, then, are the ten basic guidelines I suggest that every family follow in evaluating, buying and managing an investment portfolio. As you can see, many of these principles are closely related to the principles of the underground economy that have already been discussed. I'm strongly in favor of practices like prior planning and bringing the whole family into the investment process. And I'm totally opposed to excessive debt and risking all your holdings through such unwise practices as assuming personal liability. Each of these investment principles can be traced back to qualities that many early Americans employed in building their own wealth. And these guidelines are equally applicable today.

In the course of discussing these guidelines, a number of examples of investments have been included. But in order to design a complete investment portfolio, it's necessary to get much more specific. Now it's time to evaluate all the major kinds of investments available today in terms of their risk and return and to consider which types might be most useful for you and your family.

CHAPTER TWELVE

===

The Complete Underground Investment Portfolio

We are now ready to consider a variety of specific investments, but as this discussion proceeds, it's extremely important to keep in mind the ten guidelines in the previous chapter. You have a special, individual set of needs, and only you can make the final decision about the best kinds of assets for your portfolio. Those ten guidelines will help you exercise good judgment and also tailor an investment strategy that will suit your unique situation.

As we go through these investment opportunities, we'll be looking at them in terms of the *risk and return* standard already discussed—but with one major addition: It will be helpful at this stage to assign a numerical value according to the relative amount of risk and return for each type of investment. That way, you'll be better able to compare different assets to see what advantages or disadvantages they may offer you, given your specific financial goals and needs.

But before we go further, a few definitions are in order: First of all, both income and growth are included under the general term *return*. *Income* means the average, current yearly income an investment yields; and *growth* refers to the average yearly appreciation of the underlying equity or capital you have in an investment. So, you may get 12 percent a year income from a savings account in a bank, but no growth because your initial capital investment remains constant. And you may get 20 percent a year growth from a piece of farmland you own, but no income because it's not under cultivation at present or being rented out.

The term *risk* refers to the potential loss, either partial or total, which you are likely to sustain because of the relative security or insecurity of your investment. For example, a government treasury bill may be virtually risk free (in the present economy) because the only way you would lose it would be for the government to collapse. But the commodities market may involve an extremely high risk because the products you're likely to buy are quite volatile in price.

To measure return (income and growth) and risk, I've devised a scale from zero to ten that can be applied to each investment. Zero represents the least risk or return, and ten represents the most. Thus, an investment with an income and growth potential of 0 and a risk factor of 10 would represent the worst possible investment, while income and growth of 10 and risk of 0 would be the best.

Finally, for the easiest kind of evaluation and comparison, the investments are divided into three basic categories: income, growth, and speculative investments.

The *income* category of investments may also have some underlying growth potential. But I've put investments under this classification if their primary strength is ordinary income potential.

The *growth* investment group includes those selected primarily for their long-term appreciation (usually three years or more). Current income may also be generated by these investments, but normally the income only covers investment overhead. The risk evaluation for these growth investments takes into account the investment's ability to make its own payments beyond the initial capital outlay. Thus, a financed investment with no income potential would be rated a higher risk than one that could generate some income.

Finally, the last category is *speculative* investments. These have been selected in light of their potential for generating capital gains income in three years or less. The important consideration with these assets is weighing the potential return against the risk—with little regard for current income potential.

The assets under each of these three categories will also be discussed in light of many of the other factors we've examined in this book—such as the likelihood of a future monetary crisis, and the importance of grounding every aspect of personal money management on the great spiritual and economic principles of our past. Of course, these evaluations are presented to *aid* the potential investor in devising a complete portfolio suitable to his or her needs. But these suggestions shouldn't be accepted as absolutes. Times and economic conditions are constantly changing, and investments change along with them.

INCOME INVESTMENTS

1. U.S. GOVERNMENT SECURITIES

ASSETS: The treasury bills and other U.S. government securities in this category are very secure and, as of this writing, offer a return of 7 percent to 15 percent annually.

LIABILITIES: The fact that they offer fixed income which will probably often run below the inflation rate means that the investor's buying power will constantly shrink. Also, the principal invested in these accounts doesn't grow, so the initial capital investment will steadily get smaller through the effects of inflation. If there is a monetary crisis and the government steps in to put severe restraints on our economy, the capital account may be frozen and withdrawals of principal prohibited for an indefinite period. But the income will probably keep coming in and the principal, even if temporarily unavailable, will be safe (unless the government itself falls). Finally, 100 percent of the income from this investment is taxable as ordinary income, and the principal is illiquid, with requirements of large initial investments and severe penalties for any withdrawal before the maturity date.

EVALUATION: Income = 5; Growth = 0; Risk = 1.

2. BANK SECURITIES.

ASSETS: This category includes short-term passbook accounts and long-term certificates of deposit in banks, with an annual interest range from 5 percent to 15 percent in times of high interest rates. They require less initial investment than high-interest government securities, with $10,000 usually the minimum for the most attractive rates.

LIABILITIES: The problems are that they offer no growth of capital, the income is 100 percent taxable (with the exception of $1,000 from savings and loans), and there is no liquidity in case you want to pull your money out and put it somewhere else. (The exception to this is day-of-deposit, day-of-withdrawal accounts, which offer liquidity but the lowest interest rates.) The return on these accounts often runs behind the inflation rate, so the investor's buying power from the interest is constantly being eroded. Although many people feel comfortable when they hear that the Federal Deposit Insurance Corporation is "protecting" their investment, as a practical matter the government has less than 1 percent collateral to back up the billions of dollars of deposits in the nation's banks. If there is a wave of big bank failures, I have a serious question about whether the federal government could or would step in to cover all the losses.

EVALUATION: Income = 4; Growth = 0; Risk = 5-6.

3. MUNICIPAL BONDS.

ASSETS: These are obligations to repay issued by local municipalities around the country. They offer tax-free income, with an annual return of about 6 percent to 10 percent. It's best to buy these when they are secured by some revenue-generating asset of a city. For example, I helped one couple get into some bonds tied to city garbage trucks in Colorado so that if they didn't get paid, they could repossess the trucks. But since the trucks generate revenue for the city, the probability is that the city would pay on those bonds before many others. Hospital and road bonds offered by municipalities are also relatively safe.

LIABILITIES: They have a low yield, require large initial investments, are illiquid in that you have to agree to leave your money in for long periods of time, and offer no growth. Also, you have to be very careful about the municipality you choose because many of our larger cities are on the verge of bankruptcy.

EVALUATION: Income = 5-7; Growth = 0; Risk = 5-9. (Unless you buy a municipal bond fund which would give you enough diversity to reduce your risk factor to a 3-5 rating.)

4. FIRST MORTGAGES.

ASSETS: This investment involves a purchase by the individual of a discounted mortgage from banks or other lenders. You may get a 15 percent to 20 percent return or even more on your money, and it's a very secure asset since it's backed by the underlying property. If the borrower fails to pay, you can foreclose on the property. My advice to those who want this kind of asset is never lend an amount that exceeds more than half the value of the property. In this way, the property can drop by as much as half its original value and you'll still be protected if you have to foreclose.

LIABILITIES: The return is 100 percent taxable as ordinary income. There will be no growth of your principal, and in a rapidly inflating economy, that's a major drawback. Your investment is large, illiquid and long-term—the life of the mortgage may run from twenty to thirty years.

EVALUATION: Income = 8-9; Growth = 0; Risk = 3-4.

5. CORPORATE BONDS.

ASSETS: Bonds are issued by corporations as a first-line liability to finance their operations. The corporation is in effect borrowing from members of the public who buy its bonds, and the bonds must be paid on time by law. If a company misses three payments, it can be thrown into bankruptcy. Bondholders must also always be paid before stockholders. The return on a good bond may vary from 10 percent to 15 percent, but the amount of return depends on the rating of the bond. "C" bonds, the worst, often pay the most, while the best, "AAA" bonds, pay much less. I always recommend that my clients get high-grade bonds despite their lower return because they offer greater security. Also, I prefer those bonds which generate current income through their business operations, as do utility bonds. And I like those utility bonds that have the means of generating their own power or have access to their own coal mines or other natural resources. Bonds that are secure in this way have a much better chance of making it unscathed through a currency crisis.

LIABILITIES: One disadvantage of corporate bonds is that their income is 100 percent taxable. Also, they hold out no hope of growth for your invested capital unless inflation drops drastically and the interest paid generally on bonds drops below what you're getting for yours. Finally, they usually require a relatively large investment of a minimum of seven to ten years. It should be noted that discounted bonds (those sold at less than face value) can generate capital gains income. The difference between the face value payback and purchase price is a capital gain.

EVALUATION: Income = 7.8; Growth = 0; Risk = 5-6. (Investments in bond funds, with diversification, lower risk to 3-4.)

6. INSURANCE, ANNUITIES.

ASSETS: The few advantages of investments in insurance and annuities are that they provide tax-deferred income at a low monthly investment, your investment remains fairly liquid in that you can take it out if you need it, and you can borrow against the cash value of your insurance at generally low rates of interest.

LIABILITIES: The negatives of insurance investments are far greater than the positives. In fact, an investment in any kind of insurance is a poor investment. Insurance may have been an attractive haven for money in the Great Depression of the 1930's, but our economy and the nature of the insurance business has changed a great deal since then.

The returns on these investments have generally run about 4 percent to 6 percent though some have gone higher in recent years in an effort to compete with high-interest money-market certificates. But the return on insurance and annuities still runs less than what you can get through other fixed income investments, and there is no possibility of a decent growth rate on your principal.

There are myriads of options available with the insurance type of investment. Almost all the incentives involve borrowing paid-in premiums to be able to reinvest in higher-yield assets while deducting the interest payments. These are often attractive to those in relatively high tax brackets. But I prefer to reduce taxes through *positive* tax shelters, such as tax credits, depreciation, gifts, etc., as opposed to negative shelters, such as interest payments. Interest is negative since the government does not return as much as was paid in to the lender.

EVALUATION: Income = 2-3; Growth = 0; Risk = 5-6.

7. STOCK DIVIDENDS.

ASSETS: Common stocks that traditionally pay relatively high dividends have an advantage in that they can be purchased for a relatively small initial sum of money. For example, you can keep your brokerage fees to a minimum by buying a "whole lot" of 100 shares of a stock for whatever the quoted price per share is on the listed stock exchanges. So, if the stock you're interested in is selling for $20 a share, you can buy a whole lot for $2,000 plus the broker's commission. These investments are quite liquid in that you can put in a "sell" order to your broker, have it executed on the same day and get your money in a week or so. The return on stable income-producing common stocks has run in the range of 7 percent to 10 percent in recent years.

LIABILITIES: The problems with relying on stock dividends for income far outweigh the advantages, however. For one thing, all stock dividends are ultimately dependent on company profits, and just because a corporation has paid dividends for decades doesn't mean it will continue to do so. For example, almost no one would have believed that General Motors or Ford would reduce their dividends, but they did so when the auto industry fell upon hard times recently. One of the big problems with stock dividends is that when a person needs the income the

201

most—as during a serious economic downturn—that's just the time the corporation, under severe pressure itself, may decide to cut or eliminate dividends.

Remember: Bondholders must be paid before stockholders, so if corporate income dries up, stockholders are the first to be hurt. Finally, stock dividends are 100 percent taxable after they exceed the annual exclusion of $200 for taxpayers filing separately or $400 for married taxpayers filing jointly.

EVALUATION: Income = 6-7; Growth = 0-5; Risk =7-9.

8. MONEY FUNDS.

ASSETS: Money-market funds, which may be set up by such organizations as brokerage firms, mutual fund companies, and savings and loan banks, are an excellent place to park short-term money as you're waiting for a good investment to come along. The interest they pay varies in direct proportion to the inflation rate in the country but usually trails inflation—except when high interest rates are used to slow the growth of the money supply. So even though with a money fund you may be getting a relatively good return—and a much better return than you could get in a savings bank—you'll still be losing buying power. In recent years, these funds have ranged between about 8 percent and 20 percent annually. Other advantages of the funds are that they require relatively small minimum investments ($500 to $5,000), and they are quite liquid in that with a phone call or letter you can get your money transferred to your bank account almost immediately.

LIABILITIES: Although these funds are probably safer than banks because they spread your money among a variety of income-producing investments, they would be vulnerable to a monetary collapse. Also, the interest rate they pay is uncertain because it fluctuates with the economy. Finally, the interest is 100 percent taxable, and there is no possibility of capital growth.

EVALUATION: Income = 8-9; Growth = 0; Risk = 4-5.

GROWTH INVESTMENTS

1. DEVELOPED FARMLAND.

ASSETS: Developed farmland has consistently been the best investment over the years in the United States. And it will continue to be the best overall investment anyone can make in the future. As a result, those with a sizable surplus of money should seriously consider buying a piece of farmland debt free. In other words, if you follow the guideline presented in the previous chapter to keep one half of your investments debt free, make this the "crown jewel" of your debt-free half. But remember: Under no circumstances should you accept personal liability to acquire this or any other investment!

Developed farmland will show tremendous growth in value during the 1980's, and if you own it outright, the land will make it through any currency crisis in excellent shape. Other advantages of this investment are its relatively low cost per acre; the high demand for small tracts; and a high growth rate of 10 percent to 25 percent per year.

LIABILITIES: The investment required to buy a tract of developed farmland outright is always rather large, though the price will vary by area of the country and according to the additional development costs the buyer must sustain. Also, there is usually little or no current income from this property unless you can arrange some sort of exceptionally attractive leasing agreement.

EVALUATION: Income = 0-2; Growth = 7-10; Risk = 2-3. (If the property is financed, the risk rises to 7-8.)

2. HOUSES (SINGLE-FAMILY).

ASSETS: Single-family rental homes—and that doesn't include the home you live in—are an excellent investment. During the 1980's, single family residences will continue to grow in value in most parts of the country. There may be areas where houses will collapse in value because they are now so overvalued through local hyperinflation of real estate (for example, areas like urban California, Dallas and Seattle). But most parts of the country will offer great opportunities.

These houses require a relatively small initial investment in the form of a down payment, they provide decent current income, they offer tax shelters through depreciation and other write-offs, and they hold the promise of a good growth rate of 7 percent to 15 percent per year. (I exclude new homes with variable rate mortgages from this category because the real equity accrues to the lender.)

LIABILITIES: If you become a landlord, you have to be willing to tend to maintenance and management of your property. Also, there's always the risk that your renters won't pay the rent—and that means you'll have to start immediate eviction proceedings or sustain heavy losses through interruption of your rental income. In addition, there's the risk that you may go through lengthy periods when you can't find a renter. Finally, it takes time to find a buyer and negotiate a sale when you are ready to unload the property. And because the value of a home fluctuates with the economy, you'll have to be willing to wait for the opportune moment to put the house on the market if you hope to make a decent profit.

EVALUATION: Income = 5-6; Growth = 6-7; Risk = 4-5.

3. DUPLEXES, TRIPLEXES.

ASSETS: These are excellent investments in an economy where the inflation rate is high. These houses will be one of the best investments possible in the next five years because it's likely that larger apartment houses will be hard to build because of tight money and high costs. If you can find a well-located duplex or triplex, the chances are you'll have no trouble renting because apartment space will remain scarce in many sections of the country. There is more security in this type of rental dwelling than in the single-family house because you'll have two or more families paying you, and it's unlikely all your income will ever be cut off at the same time. Also, you can take advantage of significant tax deductions like depreciation, and you can expect a good growth rate of 10 percent a year or more on your investment.

LIABILITIES: These houses require a high initial investment and more maintenance and management than a single-family home. You're *really* becoming a landlord when you start dealing with a triplex, so if you don't think you'd like overseeing your property closely and dealing with the problems of tenants, stay away from this investment. Finally, there is a somewhat slower growth rate for this type of property, primarily because there are always more buyers around for single-family homes than for multi-family dwellings.

EVALUATION: Income = 5-8; Growth = 4-6; Risk = 3-4.

4. MUTUAL FUNDS (COMMON STOCKS).

ASSETS: Mutual funds which invest mostly in common stocks have some advantages in that they require a small initial investment. Also, fund companies usually make it possible to put small sums in regularly on a monthly basis, and they provide professional management for a much larger number of stocks than the average investor could ever buy on his own.

LIABILITIES: I don't encourage my clients to get involved with mutual funds because in general they have had poor growth records during the past decade. There are a few exceptional performers among the funds, and you can get an idea which ones they are by looking at an evaluation of their past records in the annual *Forbes* magazine mutual-fund survey or in some similar publication. But it's best not to get involved with common stock mutual funds unless you know a professional investment counselor who is good enough to direct you to a profitable one. Also, this type of investment should be left to those who want someone else to totally manage their money.

EVALUATION: Income = 1-2; Growth = 0-4; Risk = 5-7.

5. MUTUAL FUNDS (BONDS).

ASSETS: These funds have the same advantages as the common-stock funds, except that the bonds represent a credit obligation on the part of the corporations and thus offer more security than stocks.

LIABILITIES: Bond funds hold little or no promise of growth of principal, and they are also limited to a fixed payout to the extent that the return on the underlying bonds is fixed.

EVALUATION: Income = 5-6; Growth = 0; Risk = 2-3.

6. COMMON STOCKS.

ASSETS: As has already been mentioned under common-stock dividends in the Income Investments section, you can get into common stocks with a relatively small amount of initial capital. Also, there is some potential for growth—if you find the right individual stock.

LIABILITIES: Common stocks are a very poor growth investment for the vast majority of investors. Many people think they can put their money into stocks and let it sit there and grow without their having to manage it. But that's just not the case, and many people today are holding stocks that are worth only half of what they paid for them ten years ago because of the effects of inflation. Although some people are experts in common-stock investments and can consistently make money, the average investor will consistently lose. Also, he'll have no tax shelter opportunities and will earn little or no income. So I would recommend that you stay away from this investment.

EVALUATION: Income = 0-2; Growth = 0-5; Risk = 8-10.

7. GOLD, SILVER.

ASSETS: These metals can be bought either for long-term growth or for speculation, and we'll evaluate them under both categories. As for growth, both gold and silver have some significant potential. But I would lean more toward silver because gold is more likely to be confiscated by the government during a monetary crisis. Both of these metals require a relatively small initial investment, and neither requires any special management skills: You just buy it and hold onto it while watching the market for the point at which you are willing to sell. An additional asset is that the growth or increase from precious metals will be taxed as a long-term capital gain and will thus result in substantially lower taxes than earned or ordinary income.

LIABILITIES: Both metals fluctuate with the economy, with gold usually being more volatile than silver at this point. As a result, you may buy gold at a peak and have to wait years for it to reach that level again. There is no income from either of these investments, and neither offers any tax-shelter benefits. Finally, there is always a substantial resale cost, and if you try to get rid of either of these metals during a big selling period, you may have great difficulty finding a willing buyer.

EVALUATION: Income = 0; Growth = 6-7; Risk = 6-7.

8. APARTMENTS AND OFFICES (LIMITED PARTNERSHIPS).

ASSETS: Apartment and office buildings will be an excellent growth investment during the 1980's. Building and financing costs will continue to escalate so rapidly that the sooner individuals can get into one of these investments, the more opportunity they'll have to experience significant appreciation. The best way to get into big buildings with a moderate amount of money is to join a limited partnership which will enable you to pool your money with other small or medium-sized investors. As a limited partner, you limit your losses to the amount of money you've put up. These investments offer a reasonable amount of current income and also tax shelter benefits through depreciation.

LIABILITIES: Most investments of this type are purchased through large loans, with the investors putting up a relatively small amount as a down payment. But during hard economic times, tenants in apartments or offices may not pay their rent. If there are too many delinquencies, the owners may be unable to make their loan payments and have to forfeit the building. I recommend that you *never* assume personal liability with this sort of investment, even though there may be some pressure on you to do so. This is a relatively risky venture, so be sure that all you have at stake is your initial investment. Finally, the income potential from apartments and office buildings will be restricted somewhat by the necessity for you and the other owners to hire professional management and pay large, regular maintenance costs. The key here is to know the general partner and his abilities *very* well. If you don't, then don't buy in.

EVALUATION: Income = 1-5; Growth = 5-8; Risk = 6-7.

SPECULATIVE INVESTMENTS

A note of caution: These investments would normally be held by the investor for only one to three years before being resold. Also, they are to be held for the primary purpose of appreciation—not for income, though that may come incidentally. Finally, and most important, no more than 10 percent of the average investor's total portfolio should be invested in these speculative ventures.

1. GOLD, SILVER.

ASSETS: You can begin to speculate in gold and silver for a small initial investment—as little as $100. The short-term cycles of both metals are fairly predictable, because they cycle up when fear and panic rise, and then the price goes down when fear subsides. It's fairly easy to resell these metals if you develop your sales sources and don't feel compelled to unload your holdings at the worst point in the market. There is a good chance you could make 15 percent to 25 percent on your investment after commissions if you sell on a regular annual basis and get to know your outlets well. Also, if you hold onto your purchases for more than a year, you will have to pay only capital gains tax and not ordinary income tax.

LIABILITIES: Resale costs are usually high and you have to take this into account when you're calculating the growth rate of your investment. Also, the cycles in the price of gold are often long-term—perhaps a year or more —and they can be quite severe, with the metal dropping 25 percent to 40 percent in value. Finally, neither of these metals offers a tax shelter.

EVALUATION: Income = 0; Growth = 2-10; Risk = 3-4.

2. OIL, GAS EXPLORATION AND DEVELOPMENT.

ASSETS: If you can locate a reliable exploration company, I recommend these investments highly because I believe the price of both oil and gas has to go up significantly in the next five years. Also, they represent a real, tangible investment which should make it safely through any currency crisis. Oil and gas provide excellent tax shelter benefits, with 50 percent to 100 percent of the investor's investment income sheltered and the opportunity to recover around 100 percent of the initial investment in three years through tax breaks. There can also be a substantial return of 40 percent to 60 percent a year on the original investment with gas and 1,000 percent or more with oil. By proper tax management these types of investments can also be used as tremendous charitable gifts as well as tax shelters.

LIABILITIES: Although only a small percentage of most attempts to find oil and gas succeed, the success rate is much better with gas than oil. So I recommend gas over oil exploration, even though the return with oil can be much higher. One disadvantage of both oil and gas is that there is a long-term payout of return on an investment—about three years before you realize any income at all and then perhaps a couple of decades for the well to be depleted. This means there is a great deal of time for inflation to erode the value of your income. Also, most of these opportunities require a rather large initial investment, and it's hard to resell your interest in one of these wells. The key here is to invest only with *established* companies with five to ten years of track records you can verify.

EVALUATION: Income = 5-7; Growth = 0-5; Risk = 3-4.

3. COMMODITIES MARKET.

ASSETS: Commodities speculation requires a rather small initial investment and can bring in extremely high rewards —but keep reading before you get on the phone with your broker.

LIABILITIES: I've only met two or three people, among the hundreds I know who have speculated in commodities, who have made any money at it regularly. And I've also known many who have lost much more than they could afford because they bought on margin—that is, by borrowing large amounts of money from a brokerage house to finance option contracts. This is an investment which is as close to gambling as you can get because there is no way to predict the fluctuations of the market by any standard measures in the economy. So my recommendation is to stay away from this form of speculation.

EVALUATION: Income = 0; Growth = minus 10 to plus 10; Risk = 9-10.

4. COLLECTIBLES (Antiques, Autos, etc.).

ASSETS: There are a number of advantages to speculating in collectibles, and one of the most important is that you can *use* them while you're waiting to sell them. You can drive an old car, write on an antique desk, and enjoy looking at Hummel figurines on your shelves. Another advantage is that your entire family is more likely to participate in this type of investment than in any other. Also, these items seldom require a large initial outlay of money (unless you're dealing with something like extremely rare old automobiles). And if you hold any item for more than a year before you sell, you will be liable for capital gains taxes only. The annual net sales return on collectibles that are traded regularly can run 20 percent to 30 percent. The more time you devote to this business, the greater expertise you'll develop and the higher return you're likely to get.

LIABILITIES: It's extremely important that you become something of an expert in your chosen collectible field if you hope to make any money. Also, resale opportunities for most collectibles are quite limited, so you have to be in the business for a while before you become aware of the best outlets. The collectibles you hold won't generate any current income for you—there will only be return on capital growth when you sell. And there is often a long-term payout on the initial investment because an individual may have to wait years before a suitable buyer appears. In addition, the demand for collectibles fluctuates inversely with the health of the economy: When hard times hit our economy, the value of collectibles tends to go up, and when things start looking better, their value declines.

Finally, perhaps the greatest weakness with collectibles is that the would-be part-time dealer begins to regard them as purchases rather than investments. The husband or wife may fall in love with a figurine, car or other item that is supposed to be held for resale. As a result, eager buyers offering a good price may be turned away for emotional rather than financial reasons.

EVALUATION: Income = 0; Growth = 7-8; Risk = 5-6.

5. UNDEVELOPED LAND (RESIDENTIAL AND COMMERCIAL).

ASSETS: The advantages of this investment are that it can sometimes be used by the investor as he's waiting to sell, and it's available in small amounts. Also, there is a growing demand for all sorts of land, and returns are taxed at the lower capital gains rates if the land is held longer than a year.

LIABILITIES: A major problem with undeveloped land is that unless it happens to be situated in just the place where a developer is searching for property, the investor may have to develop it himself to make a profit. That can cost a great deal of money—as you know if you've ever had to pay for the installation of sewers, gas lines and the like. You may also put your money into a tract of isolated land and have to sit on it for years before a buyer appears. In the meantime, it's likely you'll be receiving absolutely no income—unless you've found some way to market the lumber or other natural resources.

EVALUATION: Income = 0-1; Growth = 5-6; Risk = 4-5. (If the land has been financed, the risk rises to 7-9.)

6. PRECIOUS GEMS.

ASSETS: Gems are available in small amounts, and investors can often wear them until they are sold. The net sales return on gems by dealers with a reasonable amount of expertise can range from 15 percent to 20 percent, and as long as the stones are held for more than a year, the return will be taxed at capital gains rates.

LIABILITIES: As with collectibles, dealing in gems is a specialized business and requires a certain level of experience and knowledge before it becomes profitable. Also, the holding period before resale is often rather lengthy, and the investor will realize no current income during this lull in trading. Diamonds are seldom used for speculation as their market is controlled by a few suppliers who try to keep the prices fairly stable. Diamonds are usually held to ensure protection of assets because, even though they don't appreciate spectacularly, they don't depreciate a great deal, either. Semiprecious stones like rubies, sapphires and emeralds make a better speculative investment for the average person.

EVALUATION: Income = 0; Growth = 6-7; Risk = 4-5.

These, then, are the three major categories of investment and some evaluations of specific opportunities in
each category. But how can you choose the specific spots
where you should put your own money?

I can't give you any precise, individual advice through
this book because each person's situation is a little different from that of the next person. But I can show you how
several real people have actually used the investment
guidelines in the previous chapter to accomplish their personal financial goals. In each case the decisions were made
with the eventuality of a monetary collapse in mind. The
result for them has been a complete, safe and profitable
set of investments—and I think their experience can serve
as a general model to help you successfully put together
your own portfolio.

As we're considering these actual cases, remember there
are five basic tiers, or levels, of risk and return, that a
person may choose from in setting up his portfolio: (1)
secure income, (2) long-term income, (3) growth, (4)
speculative growth and (5) pure speculation. Each of the
investments selected can be placed on one of these tiers.

CASE ONE: THE SALESMAN

The first example is a person we looked at in the last
chapter—the salesman making $40,000 plus a year, with a
wife and three kids, ten to seventeen. He has $20,000 to
invest now, with $8,000 in surplus to invest annually
thereafter. But I want to go over his situation once more
in light of the discussion we've just finished on specific
investment opportunities.

This person's goals are to set up an education fund for

his children, buy some recreation property and set aside money for his retirement. It's essential to have goals like these in mind before you sit down to think about specific investment opportunities because the goals will play an important role in determining the nature of the investments.

Here are the salesman's investment decisions in each category:

Tier One: Secure Income. He put about $4,000 in this category by using a liquid, daily money-market fund. This way, he would have access to some emergency cash if he needed it on short notice.

Tier Two: Long-term Income. He skipped this category because he was generating all the current income he needed through his job earnings.

Tier Three: Growth. He used $6,000 of his available cash to make a down payment on $25,000 worth of beach-front lots, which were financed by a mortgage that required payments of $100 per month. Through this investment, the salesman got a good growth property and also some real estate that his family could use for recreation. Even though this purchase was financed through a loan, the salesman assumed no personal liability on any note.

Tier Four: Speculative Growth. He put another $5,000 into a limited partnership that was purchasing some apartment complexes that offered a good tax shelter and some attractive long-term growth potential.

Tier Five: Pure Speculation. This investor put $5,000 into gold and silver—but he might as easily have invested the same amount in collectibles or another good speculative property with which he was familiar.

A man aged 42, wife and three children 10, 15, 17 years old. Salesman with $40,000 plus annual income. $20,000 to invest and $8,000 a year surplus to invest.

Goals: Education fund for children, recreation property and funds for retirement.

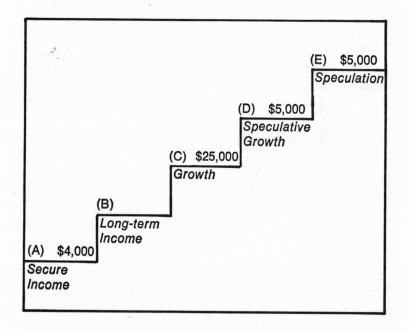

(A) Emergency cash in daily money fund at 9%–10%.

(B) No funds invested.

(C) $25,000 lake beach lots, $6,000 down payment, $100 month.

(D) $5,000 in apartment limited partnership.

(E) $5,000 in gold and silver metals.

Additional investments can be made as property in level C is paid off.

CASE TWO: THE WIDOW

This woman was forty-two years old, with two teenaged children, and she had been left $150,000 in insurance proceeds by her deceased husband. She needed an additional $8,000 a year income, above her Social Security benefits, to cover her living expenses. Her goals were to provide for her children's education and to generate extra income for her operating expenses.

Here's the way her investments came out in each of the five risk-return categories:

Tier One: Secure Income. She put $5,000 for emergency cash purposes into a daily money-market fund which would allow her to withdraw on demand whatever she needed.

Tier Two: Long-term Income. Unlike the salesman, this widow needed a steady stream of income from her investments. So she put $75,000 of her holdings into income-producing investments. Of this amount, $25,000 went into commercial paper earning about 10 percent to 12 percent over five to seven years. Another $25,000 was invested in first mortgages which yielded 14 percent to 15 percent over a twenty to twenty-five year period. And the final $25,000 went into utility company bonds, which were selected with great caution among those companies in fast-growing areas that had their own energy reserves.

Tier Three: Growth. A total of $40,000 was invested on this level. She put $15,000 into down payments on a triplex, which returns net rental income to her of 8 percent annually and will grow in value at a rate of about 10 percent to 15 percent a year. She cleans and rents this property herself, so that saves her a great deal of money in management costs. Another $15,000 went into a small farm of about 3.5 acres which she owns debt free. A share-cropper lives on the farm, and he and the widow split the proceeds from the produce. The last $10,000 went into a down payment on a rental home, which will net her 6 percent to 10 percent a year in tax-sheltered income and an equity appreciation of about 10 percent annually. Ten months' rental income from this property will cover one year's mortgage payments. I think this is a good rule of thumb for any rental property because it means that if the property goes unrented for two months out of the year, the property's own income will still cover all mortgage costs.

Tier Four: Speculative Growth. The widow invested $25,000 on this level, with the first $10,000 going into a limited partnership that buys apartment buildings. This arrangement was entered into with no personal liability on her part, and the investment was presented as having a potential of 20 percent to 25 percent growth each year. In fact, the partnership was sold in less than three years, and she realized just under $62,000 for her $10,000 investment.

She put another $10,000 into a limited partnership that

buys medical buildings, and she will get a percentage of the proceeds when the building is refinanced—something the other partners expect to do in about five years. During that time, her investment should grow at a rate of about 30 percent a year.

Finally, she put $5,000 into antiques which she bought for resale, with the idea of starting a business in this area.

Tier Five: Pure Speculation. A friend in her city was starting a salvage business, and she had a great deal of faith in his entrepreneurial abilities. So she put $5,000 into his operations, and her income from that investment is now in excess of $2,000 annually. It's also anticipated that when the business is sold in the near future, her $5,000 will be worth nearly $40,000.

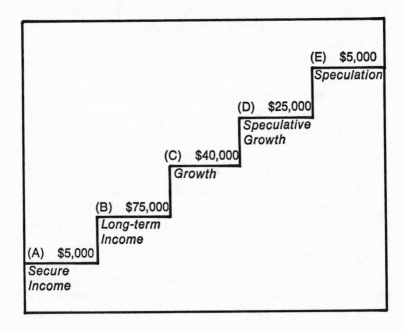

Widow, 45 years old, two teenaged children, $150,000 in insurance proceeds. Needs an additional $8,000 per year current income.

Goals: Educate children and provide for herself.

(A) Emergency cash held in daily money fund at 9%–10%.

(B) $25,000 in commercial paper at 10%–12%.
$25,000 in first mortgages at 14%–15%.
$25,000 in utility company bonds at 12%.

(C) $15,000 in triplex, average income 6%, growth 10%–15%.
$15,000 in farm land (debt free).
$10,000 in rental house, average income 5%–6%, growth 10%.

(D) $10,000 in apartment limited partnership.
$10,000 in medical building limited partnership.
$5,000 in antiques for resale.

(E) $5,000 in business venture (salvage goods).

CASE THREE: THE OLDER COUPLE

This husband and wife, who are in their early sixties, will be retiring in three to four years on a sufficient yearly income (at least at the present cost of living) from pensions and other sources. They will also have $200,000 in

221

surplus funds available for investment after selling their home and company stock.

Their goals are to have sufficient retirement income well into the future and also to preserve their surplus for travel and charitable donations.

They divided their surplus this way:

Tier One: Secure Income. They put $10,000 in money-market funds for emergency cash.

Tier Two: Long-term Income. They invested $20,000 in this category, $10,000 in first mortgages at 14 percent and $10,000 in utility company bonds at 11 percent.

Tier Three: Growth. The bulk of their surplus, $110,000, went into this category to help them preserve their assets from the threat of inflation. They put $50,000 into a condominium for themselves and another $10,000 into a rental house with an average net income of 8 percent and growth of 10 percent annually. They also invested $20,000 in mountain property which promised a growth rate of 10 percent to 15 percent a year, $10,000 in a duplex with average net income of 10 percent and growth of 10 percent to 11 percent, and $20,000 in a shopping center with an average income of 10 percent and growth of 10 percent.

Tier Four: Speculative Growth. The older couple put $45,000 of their money into investments on this level. They divided the money into equal $15,000 amounts, with the first $15,000 going into a limited partnership that bought an office complex yielding 10 percent income and 7 percent to 8 percent growth. The second portion went into a sports complex bought by a limited partnership, with the potential of 10 percent annual income and 20 percent to 25 percent growth. The final $15,000 was put in a land development company with a growth possibility of 5 percent to 20 percent annually.

Tier Five: Pure Speculation. Finally, the couple decided to invest $15,000 on this level, with $10,000 in gold and silver and another $5,000 in precious gems.

Husband and wife, early sixties. Retiring in three to four years on sufficient yearly income (at present). $200,000 surplus available with sale of home and company stock.

Goals: Retirement income and preservation of surplus to travel and give.

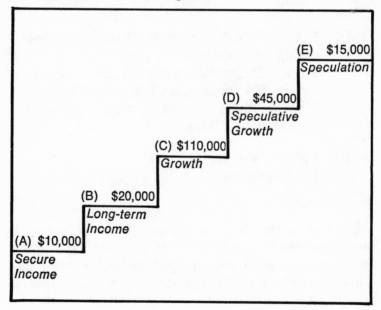

(A)   Emergency cash in daily money funds (2) at 9%–10%.

(B) $10,000 in first mortgage at 14%.
$10,000 in utility company bond at 11%.

(C) $50,000 in condominium (for self).
$10,000 rental house, average income 8%, growth 10%.
$20,000 in mountain property, growth 10%–15%.
$10,000 in duplex, average income 10%, growth 10%–11%.
$20,000 in shopping center, average income 10%, growth 10%.

(D) $15,000 in office complex limited partnership, income 10%, growth 7%–8%.
$15,000 in sports complex limited partnership, 5% income, growth 10%–15%.
$15,000 in land development company, growth 5%–20%.

(E) $10,000 in gold and silver.
$5,000 in gems.

These examples may seem somewhat unreal because I haven't mentioned any losses by these investors. And it's quite true that when you start putting money into high-risk, high-return speculative ventures, there is a real possibility of losing some or all of your investment.

But in these actual situations, the investors avoided any losses—and, in fact, made a lot of money in their purely speculative and speculative-growth decisions. The main reason for their success is that they approached their portfolio decisions logically. They moved cautiously before they put their money into anything, and they sought out expert counseling advice that had proved profitable for them in the past.

So as you put together your own portfolio, assume that you may lose a portion of your assets as you gain experience in investing. But you can also count on keeping your losses to a minimum if you follow the guidelines and the risk-return tier system that has been explained in these last two chapters. And at the same time, your potential for exceptional, inflation-beating growth will increase dramatically.

CHAPTER THIRTEEN

The Underground Economy: An Aboveground Reality

Now that we are near the end of our discussion, you can see that the underground economy is really a combination of the old and the new.

There are many traditional economic values that have been neglected in our society—values that can be traced back to the early days of this nation and even beyond that to our biblical roots. But in past times, there often wasn't a separation between a person's finances and the other aspects of his life. Personal money management was an integral part of family and community life, and all those important elements of a person's existence interacted and reinforced one another.

In the foregoing pages we have seen how ancient principles of budgeting, storing emergency food supplies, nonmoney exchange systems, community ties, self-employment ventures and investing can still be applied successfully today. But at the same time, social and economic conditions today aren't quite what they were yesterday.

For one thing, social and economic structures are much more complex now than they were even a hundred years ago. Government intervention in our lives has changed the specific applications for many personal financial principles. And there are many more investment opportunities —like the stock market, the commodities exchange and money-market funds—that were not open to our ancestors. Also, the special kind of currency collapse that we are confronting is not quite like anything that threatened our forebears because times and the challenges they bring have changed. In addition, any future collapse will affect the entire world. So it's important for the successful investor to become acquainted with the new forms—but to learn to evaluate them in terms of the old, tried and true values and standards.

That's what getting into today's legal underground economy is all about: The key thing is first to identify the important traditional principles of economic relationships. Then, it's important to use those principles as tools to organize your finances, protect yourself against a possible monetary crisis, create a surplus and turn that surplus into as large and strong a personal investment fund as possible.

This affirmation of sound personal economic concepts —with an application of financial truths to more general spiritual values—has been an important part of our traditions since biblical times. For example, Jesus drew heavily on economic illustrations to make broader points—as when he taught in Luke 14:27–30, "Whoever does not bear his own cross and come after me, cannot be my disciple. For which of you, desiring to build a tower, does not first sit down and count the cost, whether he has enough to complete it: Otherwise, when he has laid a foundation, and is not able to finish, all who see it begin to mock him, saying 'This man began to build, and was not able to finish.'" (RSV)

The point here is that the principles that will work in your personal finances will work in other aspects of your life as well. There are divinely ordained principles that underlie a successful economic as well as spiritual life. Submitting to the extent that we are able to God's will, cultivating meaningful personal relationships, looking upon our possessions not as our own but as something we hold in trust for God's work and for the benefit of other human beings—these are just a few of the spiritual values that, if affirmed, can mean the difference between success or failure, happiness or misery, peace or fear in the economic realm.

So my final word would be, make the underground economy an open and above-ground reality in your life. Recapture those fundamental, important principles of living that so much of our society has lost. If you do, perhaps you'll be on your way to sharing the blessings that the prophet Isaiah in Isaiah 66:12 says will go to Jerusalem: "For thus says the Lord: 'Behold, I will extend prosperity to her like a river, and the wealth of the nations like an overflowing stream . . .'"

I would like to thank all of the people who helped make this book a reality by both their input and tolerance. First and foremost is my wife, Judy, who encouraged me to do it, knowing that I turn into a grump while writing. Also my thanks go out to Bill Proctor who continually prodded me to finish on time. And to my staff at Christian Financial Concepts who verified and commented on many last-minute changes.

Above all else I acknowledge our Savior, Jesus Christ, for the inspiration and guidance without which this would be just a collection of words answering questions that most people never ask.

Lastly I would acknowledge our American ancestors who gave us the soundest economic and political system the world has ever seen. As bright as many of them were, it's clear that both our political and our economic systems were inspired by a much greater source of wisdom. I sincerely hope that this book will play a small part in returning us to the same type of economic society that made us great.

INDEX

INDEX

233

INDEX

INDEX